# CATAN

## PUZZLE BOOK

Unless otherwise noted, all images are courtesy of
Michael Menzel.
Dover Publications icons used as backgrounds throughout.
Shutterstock: 4-5 background, 24 bottom right, 26 top
right, 40 top right, 58-59 background, 60 background, 70
background, 71 top left, 75 top, 79 background, 87 bottom,
89 centre, 89 bottom right, 100 background, 104 bottom right,
132 background, 134-135 background, 134-135 bottom.

Published in 2020 by Welbeck
An imprint of Welbeck Non-Fiction Limited,
part of Welbeck Publishing Group
20 Mortimer Street
London W1T 3JW

10 9 8 7 6 5 4 3 2

A CIP catalogue for this book is available from the British
Library.

ISBN 978-1-78739-390-5

Printed in Dubai

# PUZZLE BOOK

EXPLORE THE EVER-CHANGING WORLD OF
CATAN IN THIS PUZZLE-SOLVING ADVENTURE

RICHARD WOLFRIK GALLAND

WELBECK

# CONTENTS

# The World of CATAN

Welcome! Whether you are already familiar with the CATAN board game, or this is your first CATAN experience, we hope you enjoy this exciting and challenging puzzle journey set on the island of Catan. If you are new to CATAN, never fear! You don't need to know the rules of the board game to enjoy these riddles and puzzles set on the fictional island of Catan.

## About CATAN

CATAN is a strategy board game that has introduced millions to the wide world of tabletop games and helped usher in the modern board game renaissance. After releasing *The Settlers of Catan* in Germany in 1995, game designer Klaus Teuber won the Spiel des Jahres (Game of the Year) award for what proved to be a revolutionary and enduring brand that has sold more than 30 million games and has been published in more than 40 different languages.

If you're ready to explore the exciting world of CATAN, here are some suggestions to get you started!

## CATAN Base Game

The enduring success of CATAN lies in the approachable mechanics and strategy, which are attractive to all levels of players; it takes minutes to learn yet offers challenges for even the most seasoned strategist.

## CATAN® – Seafarers

If you already have the CATAN base game and are ready for something a little more advanced, the next stop on your voyage should be *CATAN® – Seafarers*, an expansion that adds new elements of gameplay and variability but not too many new rules. *Note: This CATAN expansion requires a copy of the base game to play.*

## CATAN Dice Game

A fun, fast-paced roll-and-write game that goes where boards can't. With double-sided score sheets, there are two different ways to play this game. Take it on your next restaurant outing, a picnic, or other locations where a board and pieces aren't practical.

## CATAN® – Starfarers

If you're ready for something a little more out-of-this-world, traverse the galaxy with *CATAN® – Starfarers*. With elements of beloved CATAN gameplay, you'll explore the universe, befriend alien civilizations, and earn fame as you settle unexplored solar systems.

# Introduction

Over the course of the *CATAN® – Puzzle Book* you must lead a group of intrepid settlers through a series of difficult challenges. These begin with the discovery of a bountiful, untouched land, and progress as you endeavour to develop a brave new society, co-existing peacefully with other nearby settlements.

As with the board game, as you solve the various puzzles that afflict your budding band of workers and tradesmen you will earn resources and achievements. When you solve a CATAN Puzzle, you will be rewarded with a resource (LUMBER, ORE, WOOL, GRAIN or BRICK) or, on some rare occasions, an achievement (ROADS, SETTLEMENTS, CITIES and KNIGHTS).

In the grids below, you can mark each puzzle as complete when you have solved it and tally your resources and achievements. While some achievements can be gained from simply solving a puzzle, you must also build some from resources you have earned, as follows:

**Road** – 1 brick + 1 lumber
**Settlement** – 1 brick + 1 lumber + 1 wool + 1 grain
**City** – 3 ore + 2 grain
**Knight** – 1 ore + 1 wool + 1 grain

Of course, building costs resources. Once you have used a resource you must remove it from your tally. Cities can only be built upon existing settlements; you cannot, for example, have three cities but only two settlements. Similarly, never forget the importance of infrastructure to the peaceful expansion of your young nation! For every settlement or city you have – more than your first – you must have two roads. For example:

**1 settlement** – no roads needed
**2 settlements or cities** – 2 roads needed
**3 settlement or cities** – 4 roads needed

And what does this all achieve? Victory points, of course! Just as in the board game, if you win 10 victory points, then you have "won" the book. Never fear, just as it is impossible to play the perfect game, you need not complete every puzzle correctly to achieve this. Strategy is all important. Victory points are achieved as follows overleaf:

**Road** – 1 victory point for every 5 roads built
**Settlement** – 1 victory point for every settlement built (a maximum of 5 can be built before the island runs out of space!)
**City** – 2 victory points for every settlement built (a maximum of 5 can be built before the island runs out of space!)
**Knight** – 1 victory point for every three knights gained

## Good luck, and happy puzzling!

**COMPLETED PUZZLES**

| | | | | | | | | | |
|---|---|---|---|---|---|---|---|---|---|
| 1 | 2 | 3 | 4 | 5 | 6 | 7 | 8 | 9 | 10 |
| 11 | 12 | 13 | 14 | 15 | 16 | 17 | 18 | 19 | 20 |
| 21 | 22 | 23 | 24 | 25 | 26 | 27 | 28 | 29 | 30 |
| 31 | 32 | 33 | 34 | 35 | 36 | 37 | 38 | 39 | 40 |
| 41 | 42 | 43 | 44 | 45 | 46 | 47 | 48 | 49 | 50 |
| 51 | 52 | 53 | 54 | 55 | 56 | 57 | 58 | 59 | 60 |
| 61 | 62 | 63 | 64 | 65 | 66 | 67 | 68 | 69 | 70 |
| 71 | 72 | 73 | 74 | 75 | 76 | 77 | 78 | 79 | 80 |
| 81 | 82 | 83 | 84 | 85 | 86 | 87 | 88 | 89 | 90 |
| 91 | 92 | 93 | 94 | 95 | 96 | 97 | 98 | 99 | 100 |

## RESOURCES

**Lumber**

**Ore**

**Wool**

**Grain**

**Brick**

## Roads

## Settlements

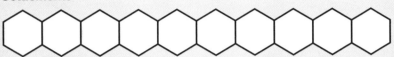

## Cities

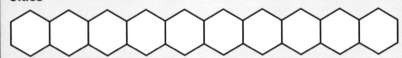

## Knights

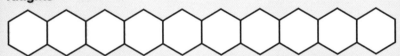

 Mountains

 Field

 Hills

 Forest

 Pasture

 Sea

 Ore

 Grain

 Brick

 Lumber

 Wool

 Desert

# PART 1: DISCOVER

The world is vast and full of wonder, or so they say. For as long as you can remember you have dreamed of leaving the confines of your birthplace and finding somewhere to start a new life. A better life.

Your first great discovery was that others shared your vision and you would not have to follow your dream alone. Shipbuilders and traders, woodcutters and shepherds all flocked to your banner. Soon you had an impressive band of settlers, eager to risk everything and explore the unknown in their search for a new home.

**"It is with an iron will that they embark on the most daring of all endeavors... to meet the shadowy future without fear and conquer the unknown."**

– Ferdinand Magellan

# 1. Landfall

Your journey has begun! With a crew of eager seafarers and enough provisions for several months at sea, you set sail in pursuit of a new world.

The voyage is not without incident, and, after eight weeks of timber-torturing tempests, seasickness and unreliable navigation, you find yourself becalmed, low on food and quite lost.

Just as you are starting to despair of ever setting foot on solid ground again, the ship's look-out calls "Land ho!" You have discovered an island!

And what an island it is. Scouts are sent out to get the lay of the land. The roughly hexagonal regions are a curiosity, but stranger still is the topography of the island's coastline. The formations seem natural, but you feel certain you can discern a pattern in the orientation of the different terrains.

Only one region remains uncharted. However, when your scouts return, they bring back six different reports!

**Would any of the hexagons to the right (a–f) fit into the uncharted region? If so, which one?**

Solution
p.178

If you completed the map, add
**1 SETTLEMENT**
to your achievements

# 2. First Impressions

Having decided on a place to settle, it's time to look for vital resources. You assign your hardiest scouts to this task: Bjorn, Frigg and Morgana.

  All three scouts return at sunset, exhausted and excited, having made a series of discoveries at different times of the day and in different locations. You must unravel their discoveries from the following clues:

– A vein of ore was discovered in the centre of the island.
– Morgana made her discovery early in the morning.
– The woodland source of lumber was not discovered at noon.
– Bjorn explored the south of the island before Frigg made her discovery.
– The north was not explored in the evening.

**Can you determine which direction each scout took, which resource they discovered and at what time they made their discovery?**

**Solution
p.178**

If you solved the
puzzle, add
**1 LUMBER**
to your resources

|  | Morning | Noon | Evening | Brick | Ore | Lumber | Frigg | Bjorn | Morgana |
|---|---|---|---|---|---|---|---|---|---|
| **North** | | | | | | | | | |
| **Centre** | | | | | | | | | |
| **South** | | | | | | | | | |
| **Frigg** | | | | | | | | | |
| **Bjorn** | | | | | | | | | |
| **Morgana** | | | | | | | | | |
| **Brick** | | | | | | | | | |
| **Ore** | | | | | | | | | |
| **Lumber** | | | | | | | | | |

| Scout | Direction | Time | Resource |
|---|---|---|---|
| | | | |
| | | | |
| | | | |

**TIP**

This is a classic logic puzzle: put a tick in a box when you have confirmed a piece of information and a cross in any of the boxes you know to be false. For example: if the North were explored in the morning, put a tick in the box intersected by "North" and "Morning" and put crosses in "North/Noon", "North/Evening", "Centre/Morning" and "South/Morning".

# 3. Agriculture

Now that you have established your first settlement, you must consider your settlers' basic needs. You have discovered that the island has rich soil and is replete with edible flora. Nevertheless, you must create a sustainable source of food if you want your people to survive. Cultivating the land and raising crops is the first step toward growing your community.

In the grid opposite are 15 words relating to (and including) GRAIN. The words can run horizontally, vertically or diagonally, forwards or backwards.

## Find all 15 words to feed your people!

Here are some clues to help you find the words. The number of letters is in brackets.

1   A cereal grain used for animal fodder and malted to make beer (6).
2   The hard, outer layers of cereal grain – a good source of fibre (4).
3   Any grass cultivated for its edible grain – and a popular breakfast (6).
4   Another word for maize (4).
5   Collective word for harvested plants (4).

6   To raise or grow plants (9).
7   A powder ground from raw grain (5).
8   The embryo of a cereal seed (4).
9   The seed of a cereal (5).
10  The gathering of crops (7).
11  The seed and husk of a cereal – not a military rank (11).
12  Good food for livestock and a healthy "meal" for humans (3).
13  A building where you grind grain (4).
14  To plant seeds by scattering (3).
15  The most widespread type of cultivated grass (5).

| | | | | | | | | | | | | | | |
|---|---|---|---|---|---|---|---|---|---|---|---|---|---|---|
| C | L | T | L | V | Z | B | D | C | C | O | G | G | C | S |
| L | G | C | L | W | L | W | L | O | C | D | Q | E | S | P |
| U | X | R | Q | M | I | I | E | R | H | S | K | C | R | H |
| V | B | O | S | J | N | B | D | N | T | N | D | V | F | M |
| Z | L | P | S | D | S | P | T | E | X | M | L | G | R | L |
| V | T | V | W | W | D | O | T | U | K | I | R | U | E | H |
| H | H | S | M | X | E | A | W | P | Z | L | O | N | Q | A |
| X | Y | G | P | T | V | D | W | B | L | L | R | D | B | R |
| J | Y | Z | R | I | L | S | U | T | F | E | M | M | O | V |
| W | X | A | T | A | B | A | W | B | K | V | T | F | A | E |
| Y | H | L | G | J | I | P | J | A | G | W | H | E | U | S |
| F | U | E | R | H | F | N | Q | R | G | B | U | C | V | T |
| C | N | X | A | Y | J | B | K | L | J | F | R | Q | J | O |
| T | T | M | C | T | C | E | R | E | A | L | S | A | H | A |
| Y | C | G | X | I | B | U | C | Y | U | C | J | H | N | T |

**Solution
p.179**

If you found
all 15 words, add
**1 GRAIN**
to your resources

# 4. The Merry Lumberjacks

To construct shelters and other buildings for your settlers, you will need lumber. Fortunately, you have three very competent woodcutters in your outpost: Agnar, Ingeborg and Jarl. Wasting no time, you send them out into the huge, inviting forest to cut down the exact number of trees you need, which you task them to do before sunset.

After a productive day, the woodcutters report back to you. Unfortunately, they have quaffed a few "refreshing beverages" after their excursion, so their statements are rambling and not one hundred percent accurate.

"I cut down eighteen trees," says Agnar.

"Well, at least I didn't cut down the fewest trees," says Ingeborg.

Agnar nods admiringly at Ingeborg. "I cut down four fewer trees than you did."

Jarl joins in, "I must admit that I chopped down fewer trees than Agnar."

Agnar responds, "Yes, I cut down two more trees than you."

Ingeborg frowns. "I know the difference between the trees I cut down and the number that Jarl cut down was six."

Jarl exclaims, "I remember now! Agnar cut down twenty trees!"

Ingeborg turns to Jarl and says, "And you cut down twenty-four."

Jarl replies to Ingeborg, "You cut down six more trees than Agnar."

**Each woodcutter has made three statements. In each case, two were true but one was false. Can you untangle this information to determine how many trees each has cut down?**

**Solution
p.180**

If you discovered the truth, add
**1 LUMBER**
to your resources

Solution
p.181

If you solved
the puzzle, add
1 WOOL
to your resources

# 5. Neighbourhood

Your settlement is still just a collection of hastily constructed huts, but they are sturdy and weatherproof.

Unfortunately, any hope you had that your settlers could live side-by-side without complaint is quickly dashed. The shepherds cause the first problems when they tell you that they dislike "towns" and would rather sleep under the stars. A day later, they have headed off to the green pastures to be with their flocks.

This leaves 12 huts unoccupied, which you must divide between the remaining factions: the woodworkers, ore miners, brickmakers and farmers.

**Below is a plan of the neighbourhood. Can you divide it into four equal sections of the same shape with the same number of huts in each?**

# 6. Svart Mountain

At the centre of the island towers a titanic mountain of black rock that the settlers have named "Svart Mountain". You have hopes that the mountain is a source of much-needed ore.

Frigg, a veteran prospector, is tasked to journey to and explore Svart Mountain. She departs from your settlement at sunrise, finding a path through the forests, pastures and hills to arrive at the foot of the mountain, where she makes her notes by the light of the full moon.

After a night sleeping under the stars, Frigg begins her return journey just as the new day is dawning. She makes better time, using precisely the same route, and arrives back at the settlement in the early evening to give you her report.

**Is there any point during Frigg's return journey where she will be at the same location at the exact same time of day as on her outbound journey? How can you be sure?**

**Yep, abundant veins of ore here. Recommend sending a mining expedition ASAP.**

**Solution p.181**

If you solved the puzzle, add
**1 ORE**
to your resources

# 7. The Ship Race

Your leadership of the settlement is stressful, but comes with some perks. Chief among them is that you live in the finest house in the young town. However, your ownership has been contested by Magnus the trader, a wealthy investor who has purchased the fastest ship in your small fleet and now wants to add your house to his investments. Losing the house will not only weaken your status as leader, but also lead to a less comfortable night's sleep after a hard day's work!

However, you agree to the contest and, in return, challenge Magnus to a ship race around the island which will decide the matter.

Magnus might be wealthy and ridiculously self-confident, but you are easily the better sailor and feel reasonably sure that you can beat him in a fair race.

However, in accordance with a pre-settlement custom, both parties may make an amendment to the challenge and Magnus is eager to make use of this rule.

"Whoever's ship comes last shall be the winner!" declares Magnus, with evident satisfaction at his own cleverness.

"Good grief, Magnus!" growls Frigg, the no-nonsense ore prospector. "Haven't we got better things to do than wait for you two to spend a year and a day at sea?"

Frigg does have a point.

You must think of a succinct amendment to the challenge that will ensure your victory.

## Can you propose a solution in less than three words?

**Solution p.181**

If you won the race, add
**1 WOOL**
to your resources from
Magnus's
stores

# 8. Pyramid Scheme

The brickmakers have been hard at work in their kilns and are finally ready to ship their first consignment of brick.

   The brick will be transported in four layers of different sizes (smallest, small, large and largest), stacked in a rough pyramid.

   Your task is to organize the transportation of the pyramid from point A to point C, moving just one layer at a time. You can move a layer between points A, B and C but there must never be a larger layer placed on top of a smaller one.

**What is the fewest moves it will take to reconstruct the pyramid at point C?**

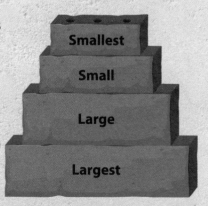

Smallest

Small

Large

Largest

Solution p.182

If you moved the bricks correctly, add 1 BRICK to your resources

# 9. Guard Duty

So far, you have encountered no hostile activity on the island beyond a few wild dogs. But that doesn't mean you can afford to be complacent.

You instruct the other settlers to get to work constructing watchtowers. These will surround the settlement like the hour pips on a clock, and every able-bodied adult will be required to take a shift on guard duty at least once a week – including you!

There are 12 sentry posts. A guard is required to stand at each post for 30 minutes before moving to the next one, which takes exactly 5 minutes.

Once a guard has finished their shift at the 12th post, it takes 17-and-a-half minutes to walk back to the settlement and get some much-needed rest.

**If you set off for work at 9 p.m., what time will you get back home?**

**Solution
p.182**

If you solved the puzzle, add
**1 BRICK**
to your resources

# 10. Mathematical Certainty

One evening, you attend the Council of Sages. The sages are, without a doubt, the wisest of your settlers, but they tend to speak in riddles and have a baffling sense of humour.

"It always comes down to mathematics," declares Frederich, the Sage of the Hills. "Not just numbers, of course, but the operators – they are key to managing our destiny."

"Yes! An addition is always welcome," agrees Michaela, the Sage of the Pasture.

"But you can have too much of a good thing," replies Frederich with a smile.

"With multiplication, we grow and prosper," chimes Barbara, the Sage of the Fields.

"But it can get crowded on a small island," says Peter, the Sage of the Forest. "Perhaps division is better. It encourages us to share."

"Or to tear ourselves apart," says Frederich.

"Subtraction then," intones Piet, the Sage of the Mountains.

The other four sages nod in solemn agreement but their eyes are twinkling with mirth.

**Why is subtraction the best function for changing the world?**

**Solution p.182**

# PART 2: EXPLORE

After making landfall, you assess your surroundings. The newly discovered area opens up to reveal more islands, more natural resources and even more places to settle!

You will now depend on your intrepid scouts to map out the outlying regions and warn you of any impending perils. It is miraculous that these lands are uninhabited. Surely it cannot be long before other explorers find this new paradise and challenge your settlers for living space.

**"What do dreams know of boundaries?"**

– Amelia Earhart

# 11. Island Hopping

You have sent out scouts to explore a cluster of nearby islands, each of which is rich in resources, except for small patches of desert. They report back three days later with a pretty thorough piece of cartography. However, they were unable to penetrate the centre of the third island.

With winter coming, you do not want to send out another expedition. Surely, with your considerable topological skills, you can determine the contents of the mysterious black hexagon.

## Which of the hexagons opposite (a–f) belongs in the centre of the third island?

Solution
p.182

If you completed the
map, add
1 ORE
to your resources

# 12. Into the Woods

Lumber is essential for your roads and settlements. The island's forests are home to a generous variety of trees that can be converted into this precious building material. Of course, being a conscientious settler, you vow to preserve the rarer species of flora and replant the woodlands as often as possible!

In the grid opposite are 15 words relating to LUMBER. The words can run horizontally, vertically or diagonally, forwards or backwards.

## Find all 15 words. Chop-chop!

Here are some clues to help you find the words. The number of letters is in brackets.

1   It grows out from a trunk or bough (6).
2   Someone who makes and repairs wooden items (9).
3   The practice of maintaining woodland areas (8).
4   The business of cutting and processing trees to produce lumber (7).
5   A North American woodcutter (10).
6   Tree associated with a sweet syrup, and Canada! (5).
7   A tree of the genus Quercus, grown from acorns (3).
8   An evergreen conifer with distinctive cones (4).
9   Rectangular lumber, walked by penalized pirates (5).
10  A place for cutting logs into lumber (7).
11  A long, thin piece of wood (5).
12  Something you shout when cutting down a tree (6).
13  A plant with a trunk and branches (4).
14  Can be a body, a chest or a nose (5).
15  The material of trees and a place where they live (4).

| | | | | | | | | | | | | | | |
|---|---|---|---|---|---|---|---|---|---|---|---|---|---|---|
| | G | X | B | N | D | P | P | Y | Q | H | E | N | H | P |
| J | R | I | R | O | Z | L | O | G | G | I | N | G | H | Q |
| B | U | U | O | M | T | A | T | P | K | X | M | O | A | K |
| | N | W | N | L | U | M | B | E | R | J | A | C | K | K |
| E | J | F | X | K | C | H | D | X | S | M | H | K | H | I |
| M | F | D | Y | C | X | N | Q | G | A | A | N | G | Q | R |
| S | P | R | B | T | O | L | B | D | V | D | X | Z | E | T |
| A | L | I | B | R | A | N | C | H | N | X | Y | T | C | I |
| W | A | B | N | E | F | Z | M | R | F | Q | N | M | E | M |
| N | N | M | G | E | S | K | V | U | K | E | K | B | X | B |
| | K | A | S | X | A | W | M | O | P | U | N | Z | R | E |
| | R | P | H | T | Z | F | O | R | E | S | T | R | Y | R |
| | U | L | W | B | I | O | A | R | C | T | E | B | C | W |
| | L | E | W | L | V | C | R | T | S | N | F | D | K | W |
| H | T | W | U | X | T | D | K | L | F | W | K | F | T | E |

**Solution p.183**

If you found all 15 words, add **1 LUMBER** to your resources

33

# 13. Out for the Count

Even as you turn your attention further afield, you must keep an eye on the day-to-day activities of your community.

Island life can bring out strange habits in the new inhabitants. Your scouts, for example, have taken to embellishing their reports with bad poetry, unnecessary details and cryptic interpretations of simple facts.

Here is an example, received after a routine check of the settlement's livestock. Your instruction, to determine how many sheep you had, was simple. The answer was not.

Your scout's note is reproduced below.

**How many sheep does the settlement have?**

I located a pasture and there I did spy,

Lambs, sheep and shepherds under the sky,

Heads two and seventy had herders and flock, And

two hundred legs of which I took stock.

**Solution
p.184**

If you deciphered the note, add
1 WOOL
to your resources

# 14. The First Harvest

Farmer Helga has two fields of equal size; one contains barley and the other wheat.

She assigns her two best hands, Sigge and Steinn, to harvest the crops before the first frosts come.

Sigge is an early riser and a rather impetuous worker. He arrives before the break of dawn and commences scything the wheat. He has cleared three hectares of the crop before his more careful colleague, Steinn, arrives.

"What time d'you call this?" says Sigge with a satisfied smirk.

"What in Catan are you doing, Sigge?" asks Steinn. "Helga said she wanted you to take care of the barley."

Sigge swallows his ire and immediately sets to work on the barley, while Steinn continues to harvest the wheat.

Steinn clears his field first, but he feels bad for Sigge and goes to help him, clearing six hectares of barley to finish the harvest.

That evening, Helga pays her hands one silver ingot for every hectare harvested.

## Who gets the most ingots and by how many?

**Solution p.184**

If you solved the puzzle, add
**1 GRAIN**
to your resources

# 15. Island Index

Sage Havardr the Wise, your self-appointed economics "expert," has published his evaluation of the smaller islands that lie off the coast of your settlement. He has marked the regions according to their production or consumption, but his algorithms make little sense to anyone else and, unfortunately, he has already set out to explore another group of recently discovered islands.

You intend to send an expedition of brickmakers to the fourth island, but you could save a lot of unnecessary time and energy if you could first ascertain whether its hills are productive.

**Can you work out the mathematical links between the resources to discover the sage's thinking and determine the value of brick on the bottom island?**

Hexagon 1:
7, 6, 2, 44, 3, 4, 3

Hexagon 2:
4, 4, 5, 60, 2, 3, 1

Hexagon 3:
5, 5, 5, 90, 5, 5, 5

Hexagon 4:
8, 1, 7, 90, 3, 2, ?

Solution p.184

If you found the value, add
**1 BRICK**
to your resources

# 16. Road Loop

Building roads requires some forward planning. It is decided that each community should have a single unbroken road loop with no dead ends. Furthermore, a main road that enters a settlement must not run straight through it, whereas one that goes through a forest must not deviate.

**Draw a single continuous line around the grid that passes through all the settlements and forests.**

**Solution
p.185**

If you complete this
road loop, add
**1 ROAD**
to your achievements

**Settlement**   **Forest**

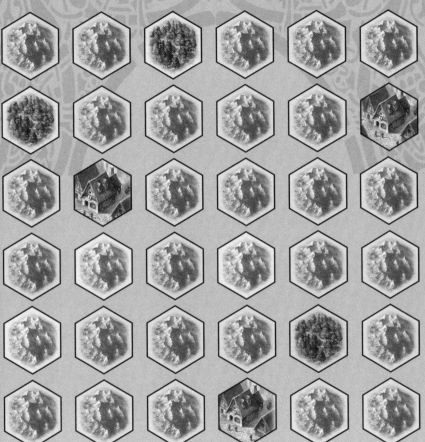

If you enter a settlement, turn left or right within the settlement hex and pass straight through the next hex you come to. Ensure that this works for both routes going in and out of the settlement.

If you enter a forest, keep going straight through the forest hex and turn left or right in the next hex. Ensure that this works for at least one route going into the forest.

# 17. The Island in the Island

Ragna, one of your finest scouts, has set out to explore the island with her faithful donkey, Grima.

Grima carries spartan provisions: an empty flask with the capacity of about 1 pint, 250 yards of rope, a 5-foot walking pole, a sack of flags and a mutton sandwich.

Heading toward the centre of the island, Ragna makes a remarkable discovery – a smaller island surrounded by a deep, circular lake. This island is bare, except for just one thing: a very rare, very valuable type of oak tree.

As a passionate conservationist, Ragna wants to protect this beautiful specimen from woodcutters' axes.

According to the Explorer's Treaty, any land surrounded by water can only be claimed by a community if a settler marks the land with their community's uniquely coloured flag.

There is just one small problem. Despite being the best climber, runner, forager and arm-wrestler in your community, Ragna forgot to mention on her scout application form that she cannot swim!

Realizing her predicament, Grima informs her with an indignant "Eee-aww!" that he is terrified of water, so don't even think about it.

Ragna tethers Grima to the only sturdy tree on the shoreline and nibbles on her mutton sandwich while pondering her surroundings. The lake has a diameter, shore to shore, of about 80 yards and the oak is an impressive 155 feet tall. When she attempts to throw a flag across the water, it plops into the lake having barely flown five yards, receiving a contemptuous snort from Grima.

Nevertheless, the following day, Ragna returns home, proudly presents an acorn from the rare oak, and announces that she has secured the island.

**How did she achieve this?**

**Solution p.185**

If you solved the puzzle, add
**1 BRICK**
to your resources

# 18. Mist Directions

To help your fellow settlers find their way around the foggy island of Caligo, you have erected numerous signposts. Each is constructed from strong lumber with letters burned and stained into wooden arrows to provide clear directions.

You are travelling from the harbour to the sacred grove of Frigga along a mercifully straight path. After an hour's walk, you come to a crossroads... just as the island's mists close around you.

To your horror you find that one of your precious signposts has been ripped out of the ground. It seems to be otherwise intact, so you have no way of knowing whether it was a natural occurrence or sabotage.

Surely, you cannot be too far from your destination, but you have no idea of the direction.

## How can you find your way to the sacred grove?

**Solution
p.186**

If you found your
way, add
**1 WOOL**
to your resources

# 19. Obscurity

The newly discovered isle of Langaholm is divided into 24 productive regions. It is notoriously hard to map the layout of these regions because a perpetual layer of thick fog covers almost all of the island's surface.

However, you do know that Langaholm produces just three types of resource: lumber from its forests, brick from its hills and grain from its fields, and the regions have been divided so that no region is adjacent to another that supplies the same resource. You also know that region 5 is a hill region, and region 9 contains fields.

## What sort of resource should be allocated to the 24th region?

**Solution p.186**

If you identified the region, add
**1 LUMBER**
to your resources

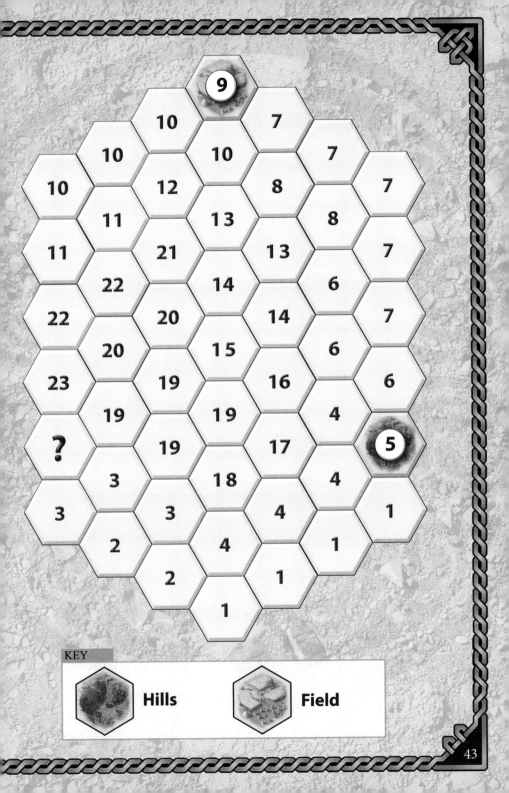

# 20. The Following Day

You will need to have completed the puzzle *First Impressions* (Puzzle 2) in order to attempt this puzzle.

The day after the scouts reported their initial findings, you dispatched three work teams to start extracting resources.

## From the clues below, can you determine who led which team, how many workers they had, which resource they were assigned to extract and what problems they encountered?

– 15 workers are assigned to the resource that was discovered yesterday morning.
– The resource discovered in the south is proving difficult to get to due to a landslide.
– Fenrir's team encounter a freak fire and are glad to have more than 10 workers to deal with it.
– Jarnsaxa leads a team of 12 workers.
– Egil will not lead the workers assigned to extract the resource discovered earlier by Frigg.

|  | 10 Workers | 12 Workers | 15 Workers | Landslide | Fire | Wild dogs | Fenrir | Jarnsaxa | Egil |
|---|---|---|---|---|---|---|---|---|---|
| Brick |  |  |  |  |  |  |  |  |  |
| Ore |  |  |  |  |  |  |  |  |  |
| Lumber |  |  |  |  |  |  |  |  |  |
| Fenrir |  |  |  |  |  |  |  |  |  |
| Jarnsaxa |  |  |  |  |  |  |  |  |  |
| Egil |  |  |  |  |  |  |  |  |  |
| Landslide |  |  |  |  |  |  |  |  |  |
| Fire |  |  |  |  |  |  |  |  |  |
| Wild Dogs |  |  |  |  |  |  |  |  |  |

| Resource | Workers | Problem | Leader |
|---|---|---|---|
|  |  |  |  |
|  |  |  |  |
|  |  |  |  |

**Solution p.186**

If you solved the puzzle, add 1 ORE to your resources

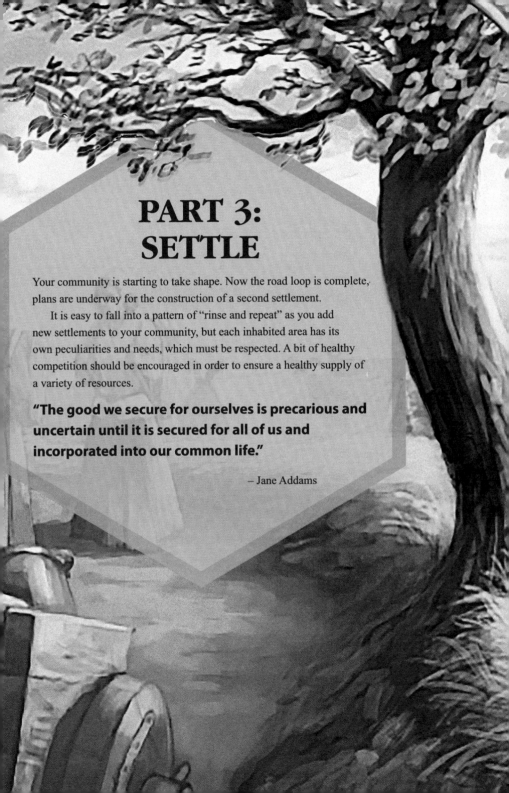

# PART 3:
## SETTLE

Your community is starting to take shape. Now the road loop is complete, plans are underway for the construction of a second settlement.

It is easy to fall into a pattern of "rinse and repeat" as you add new settlements to your community, but each inhabited area has its own peculiarities and needs, which must be respected. A bit of healthy competition should be encouraged in order to ensure a healthy supply of a variety of resources.

**"The good we secure for ourselves is precarious and uncertain until it is secured for all of us and incorporated into our common life."**

– Jane Addams

# 21. Stronger Foundations

Your scouts have discovered a new region that is rich in resources and quite close to your proposed second settlement. To your consternation, the only part they haven't surveyed is an area of hills. Once again, you will have to supplement their reconnaissance with your own powers of deduction.

The figure in each hexagon is the production level of the resource – the higher the better. You are sure there is some pattern to the production levels, but what is it?

**Can you determine the total production of brick throughout the whole region?**

Solution
p.186

If you solved the puzzle, add
1 BRICK
to your resources

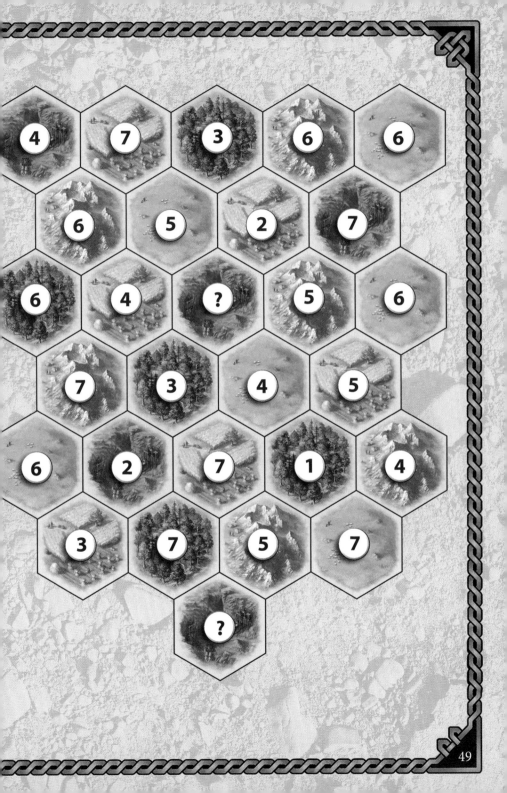

# 22. Baa!

You have brought sheep to the island and they have happily settled into its verdant pastures.

In the grid opposite are 15 words relating to (and including) SHEEP. The words can run horizontally, vertically or diagonally, forwards or backwards.

## Find all 15 words to clothe your community!

Here are some clues to help you find the words. The number of letters is in brackets.

1. The distinct wavering cry of a sheep or goat (5).
2. A female sheep (3).
3. The woolly covering of a sheep, shorn as a single piece (6).
4. A group of sheep (5).
5. Making garments from yarn with stitches and needles (8).
6. A young sheep (4).
7. The meat of older sheep (6).
8. Land used for grazing (7).
9. A male sheep (3).
10. The process of removing the fleece (8).
11. Quadrupeds of the genus *ovis* (5).
12. Someone who looks after sheep (8).
13. Twisting together fibres to make yarn (8).
14. Textile fibre obtained from sheep (4).
15. A length of interwoven fibres used in textile production (4).

| | | | | | | | | | | | | | |
|---|---|---|---|---|---|---|---|---|---|---|---|---|---|
| V | Q | P | C | F | L | E | E | C | E | N | X | J | W | K |
| S | L | N | F | L | J | F | N | O | B | C | I | P | Y | X |
| H | U | O | F | O | I | M | I | G | D | C | K | Q | P | M |
| E | C | J | Q | C | U | H | G | Y | D | X | Y | A | A | U |
| A | L | R | K | K | N | I | T | T | I | N | G | S | T |
| R | S | M | U | K | I | B | O | W | Q | A | C | W | T | T |
| I | Y | I | Q | N | J | F | E | T | A | X | U | B | U | O |
| N | M | P | N | Q | M | H | A | L | F | A | V | J | R | N |
| G | W | I | Z | Q | Z | E | P | K | L | A | I | M | E | D |
| V | P | Z | G | T | L | E | O | C | F | T | W | S | L | M |
| S | N | P | N | B | E | Y | P | K | X | X | Y | O | L | H |
| S | O | I | H | H | E | P | A | X | X | K | E | O | I | L | I |
| P | X | G | S | B | F | K | V | R | U | W | N | Z | A | O |
| M | I | R | Z | L | K | R | A | M | N | E | S | H | M | W |
| J | Z | M | V | U | S | H | E | P | H | E | R | D | B | S |

**Solution p.187**

If you found all 15 words, add **1 WOOL** to your resources

# 23. Job Creation

Solution p.188

Having chosen a good spot for your new settlement, you must appoint leaders to the resource-gathering expeditions.

Your leadership candidates are Alfbjorn, Baldr, Caecilia, Dagmaer and Eric.

You decide that no candidate should be given a job they do not want but, if they offer no preference, you will assign the candidate to a job that requires a quality they possess (like "patient" or "honest"). However, a volunteer will *always* be accepted.

If you assigned the jobs correctly, add **1 SETTLEMENT** to your achievements

**From the information below, can you match each candidate with their assigned job and the quality that they possess, and that the job requires?**

1. You need to be strong to become a miner.
2. Caecilia was voted the most fastidious member of the settlement.
3. Alfbjorn volunteers to be a woodcutter but is not particularly honest.
4. Patience is not an essential quality for someone who wants to cut down trees for a living.
5. Baldr volunteers to be a shepherd.
6. Caecilia does not want to be a farmer.
7. Baldr is not patient.
8. Dagmaer is not strong.
9. You don't need to be boisterous to be a brickmaker and Eric is certainly not boisterous.

**Qualities:** honest, patient, fastidious, strong, boisterous
**Jobs:** miner, woodcutter, brickmaker, shepherd, farmer

| Name | Quality | Job |
|------|---------|-----|
|      |         |     |
|      |         |     |
|      |         |     |
|      |         |     |
|      |         |     |

# 24. Multi-Tasking

**Solution p.188**

Most of the adult settlers are specialists in an area of resource extraction, construction or public service. However, three of your trusted advisors (Oda, Gudmund and Skjald) are good at everything!

Your challenge is to put their talents to the best possible use within the constraints of a working day.

If you found your way, add **1 GRAIN** to your resources

Each advisor can only participate in four different tasks per week and you need two advisors (no more, no less) assigned to each of the six tasks per week.

## From the list of restrictions below, can you determine who will do which tasks this week?

### Oda

If she makes bricks, she must also look after the sheep.

If she looks after the sheep, she cannot mine ore.

If she mines ore, she cannot defend the settlement.

### Gudmund

If he mines ore, he must also defend the settlement.

If he defends the settlement, he cannot make bricks.

If he makes bricks, he cannot help with the harvest.

### Skjald

If she helps with the harvest, she cannot make bricks.

If she cannot make bricks, she must defend the settlement.

If she defends the settlement, she cannot mine ore.

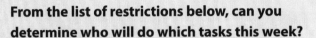

|  | Oda | Gudmund | Skjald |
| --- | --- | --- | --- |
| **Brickmaking** |  |  |  |
| **Defence** |  |  |  |
| **Harvesting** |  |  |  |
| **Ore Mining** |  |  |  |
| **Shepherding** |  |  |  |
| **Woodcutting** |  |  |  |

# 25. Black and White

Next, you must visit the two pastures that lie within your territory to check that wool production will keep your community clothed. It is two months until lambing season and the grass is covered in frost.

At the first pasture, you meet Helga, the shepherd in charge, and notice that all her sheep have black wool. She seems a little upset and reluctant to talk, even when you move the conversation to the serious business of husbandry.

"How many sheep do you have?" you ask.

"Seven," is the curt reply.

"Do you have many ewes?"

"At least half the flock are ewes."

Like most of your shepherds, Helga is an honest sort but rather taciturn, preferring the company of her woolly charges to that of other humans. On leaving her cottage, you count the flock in her pasture and satisfy yourself that there are seven sheep, just as she said.

Your second visit is almost identical to the first, except Shepherd Mimr's sheep all have white wool.

You ask him the same questions and receive a similar response:

"Nine sheep. Over a third are ewes."

Checking the flock, you count nine sheep – the correct number – and head home.

However, your advisor, Gudmund, looks troubled when you report your findings.

"I don't think our wool production is sustainable," he mutters.

## What could be the cause of Gudmund's pessimism?

**Solution
p.188**

If you discovered the problem, add
**1 WOOL**
to your resources

# 26. What's in a Name?

There are four members of your settlement whose names are a constant source of amusement: Sven the Farmer, Yrsa the Miner, Alfrikr the Shepherd and Nal the Woodcutter.

They are employed (in no particular order) as a farmer, a miner, a shepherd and a woodcutter, but the "joke" is that none of them has a surname connected to their profession.

On any night in the tavern, you can hear the same befuddled speculation about who does what:

"Sven is a woodcutter," declares one of the locals.

"Alfrikr is a farmer," says another.

"Yrsa is not a woodcutter, Sven is," says a third.

"And Nal is neither a miner or a farmer," intones a fourth customer, as if that puts an end to the matter.

You ponder these statements and conclude that Yrsa must be the miner. But that can't be right as that is her surname.

The barman smiles, clearly enjoying the game, and whispers to you, "Only one of those tipsy villagers told you any of the truth."

## Can you untangle the facts?

**Solution p.189**

If you identified the liars, add **1 GRAIN** to your resources

# 27. Mining Community

Life in the mountains is tough and the settlers who choose to live there need to be strong of body and mind.

The Miners' Guild of Stenhus originally had 200 members but 11 have already left or perished. There are concerns about the future of the mining community and you have been asked to assess its fitness.

You receive a hand-written report from the Elder of Stenhus, which has been reproduced below. You must work out a worst-case scenario for the community to determine whether there will be enough workers to extract ore from the mountain.

**What is the smallest number of potential adult volunteers who are both hardworking and healthy?**

Of our remaining settlers, 8 have stated that they will not work in the mines, 11 are children, 70 are hard workers and 140 are in a good state of health.

**Solution p.189**

If you solved the puzzle, add **1 ORE** to your resources

# 28. Ore, or...

Your inspection tour of the settlements takes you to the mines. The island's mineral deposits are impressive, but the best ore requires greater effort to extract.

The recently formed Ore Workers' Guild, a semi-secret order of miners and metalsmiths, has not been as diligent as you would like with its quality control.

You have been tipped off that one out of every nine ingots supplied by the guild is made from low-grade ore, which is slightly heavier than the desired product.

The guild's representative presents you with nine ingots with identical dimensions, and which should all weigh the same.

You have a pair of scales and a determination to present the smiling representative with a fake. But you are constrained by politics – if you take too many weighings without exposing a fake, the guild will be offended, and they might stop trading with you altogether!

## How can you locate the fake ingot in no more than two weighings?

**Solution
p.190**

If you found
the fake ingot, add
1 ORE
to your resources

# 29. The Apprentices' Test

The Order of Brickmakers have a test which all initiates must pass before they can start their apprenticeships. Each aspiring brickmaker is presented with a pyramid of blocks, with all but one block having been engraved with symbols.

The initiate is given a hammer and chisel and instructed to inscribe the single blank brick so that it completes a pattern. Once the hammer falls, there can be no going back. "Measure twice and cut once," is one of the first maxims a brickmaker learns.

To better understand the factions that comprise your community, you have asked to take this test and, as a clear sign of the Order's confidence in your leadership, they have agreed!

**Here is your pyramid. Which symbol should be etched on the blank brick?**

**Solution
p.190**

If you passed the
test, add
**1 BRICK**
to your resources

# 30. Logging

You are organizing a massive woodcutting expedition. The forest has been mapped into 64 areas and the trees that are designated to be cut down are marked with a tree symbol.

Now the woodcutters must be assigned to their trees. You consult the woodcutter's guidebook, known as "The Log," which provides strict rules:

**Distribution of labour:** No more than one woodcutter per tree, and the exact number of woodcutters on each row and column must be shown on the diagram.

**Health and safety:** 1. Each woodcutter must stand *beside* their designated tree – that is, in a neighbouring area, horizontally or vertically. 2. No two woodcutters must be *adjacent* to one another – that is, their area must not share a side or corner with another woodcutter's area.

## Can you place the woodcutters by marking their areas with a "W"?

**Solution
p.191**

If you placed the
woodcutters, add
**1 LUMBER**
to your resources

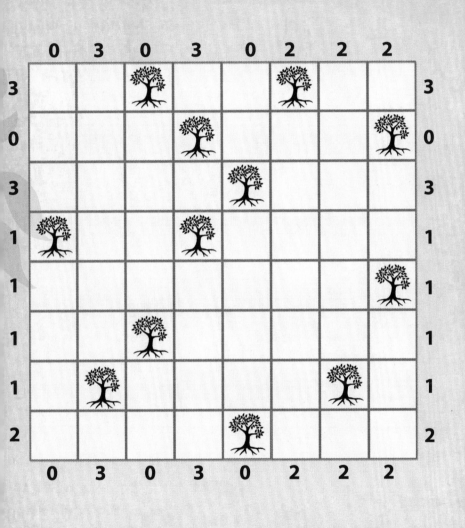

# PART 4: BUILD

Your settlements are still very young, but many of your settlers are leaving youth behind. An aging population cannot endure, so new settlers must be produced! Happily, both the Island Church and the Temple of Odin have been overworked with weddings and blessings in recent months, which bodes very well indeed.

As children enter the community, provision must be made for their schooling and welfare. There's no time to be idle on the island, and everyone must do their part.

**"We cannot always build the future for our youth, but we can build our youth for the future."**

– Franklin D. Roosevelt

# 31. New Islanders

It is a happy time indeed when a new life is brought into the community. Saga the Teacher was the first settler to give birth on the island and her children were the start of a new generation that would become acclimatized to the hardships and joys of living here.

Saga's son Bjorn is quick-witted and fond of animals. He loves to watch the shepherds tending their flocks in the nearby pasture. When asked what he would like to be when he is older, he replies, "A sheep dog!"

Bjorn's sister Eva is strong and courageous. There is nowhere she will not climb or explore; perhaps she will join the scouts or become an ore miner when she is older.

Both children like to play with their older brother, Sven, but share a very particular bond with one another. It sometimes appears as though they can communicate without talking. Sven doesn't mind this, and he takes his responsibilities as the oldest sibling very seriously.

Bjorn and Eva share the same birthday and were born in the same year. However, despite looking very much alike with their red-brown hair and sea-green eyes, they are not twins.

## How can this be?

**Solution p.191**

If you solved the riddle, add
**1 GRAIN**
to your resources

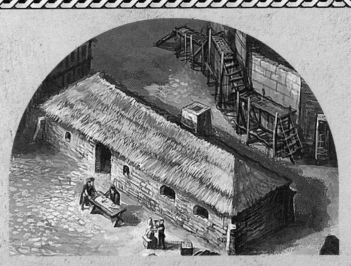

# 32. Woodcraft

The members of the Woodcraft Guild are renowned for their unique sense of humour.

When you visit the hut of Harrelson, one of your settlement's most esteemed carpenters, you brace yourself for a tirade of tall stories – or at least a sarcastic jibe – but, instead, you find him hard at work sanding down some planks.

After watching the work for several minutes with no sign of acknowledgement from Harrelson, you are compelled to ask, "What are you making?"

The carpenter looks up with a sombre, evasive expression, and you have the feeling that an oblique answer is coming.

"Something that every settlement needs," he replies, putting down his plane and picking up his pipe.

There is a flash of flint and steel, and the fragrant tang of locally cultivated tobacco blends with the aroma of sawdust and polish.

"My buyers never want one for themselves," he continues, unwilling to make eye contact. "And the recipients have no appreciation of my craftsmanship. What do you make of that?"

It is clear that Harrelson will say no more. Finishing with his pipe, he returns to his work and you leave the workshop to the lonely sound of a rasping plane.

## What item was the woodworker working on?

**Solution
p.191**

If you solved the
riddle, add
**1 LUMBER**
to your resources

# 33. Building Blocks

Brick is a vital construction material for your community. It is one of the key resources that you must ensure a steady supply of, and it is made from the clay that is fortunately abundant in the hilly regions of your island. However, your master builder can often be found poring over maps to find potential new hills to mine.

In the grid opposite are 15 words relating to (and including) BRICK. The words can run horizontally, vertically or diagonally, forwards or backwards.

## Find all 15 words to start construction!

Here are some clues to help you find the words. The number of letters is in brackets.

1. A chunk of hard material with flat surfaces (5).
2. The pattern in which bricks are laid (4).
3. A professional who can make a wall out of blocks (10).
4. An earthy material, soft when moist and hard when fired (4).
5. The process of building something (12).
6. A layer of bricks or the route of a road (6).
7. An indentation in a brick. Sounds amphibious (4).
8. A brick laid at right angles to the wall's face (6).
9. A furnace for firing pottery (4).
10. Stonework (7).
11. A paste for binding bricks (6).
12. Masonry block at the corner of a wall (5).
13. A paved route between settlements (4).
14. A brick with its long side along the face of a wall (9).
15. A continuous brick structure for keeping out unwanted guests (4).

| M | V | F | Y | A | X | W | U | R | X | D | N | V | P | Y |
|---|---|---|---|---|---|---|---|---|---|---|---|---|---|---|
| M | Q | U | O | I | N | S | E | B | L | G | B | W | N | R |
| W | X | C | A | G | X | D | B | F | I | M | J | A | L | Q |
| P | B | O | C | U | A | D | J | R | O | A | D | L | N | X |
| V | O | N | N | E | Y | Z | W | O | N | Y | Y | L | S | B |
| L | N | S | H | W | C | J | Q | G | A | O | V | I | R |
| A | D | T | Q | W | W | K | B | L | O | C | K | R | J | I |
| C | I | R | K | I | L | N | C | M | C | Y | M | R | R | C |
| M | E | U | F | U | S | D | H | C | M | O | Q | Z | Q | K |
| A | M | C | B | Z | L | J | V | A | R | F | U | L | E | L |
| S | U | T | N | U | F | I | G | A | L | S | C | R | Z | A |
| O | S | I | P | X | R | S | T | F | X | E | C | P | S | Y |
| N | S | O | E | P | X | R | N | D | K | F | K | K | D | E |
| R | A | N | D | B | O | R | W | P | H | H | S | Y | V | R |
| Y | P | I | K | M | S | T | R | E | T | C | H | E | R | U |

Solution p.192

If you found all 15 words, add **1 BRICK** to your resources

67

# 34. The Brick Road

An old prospector claims to know the location of a range of hills with a particularly fine supply of clay but tells you that the road is far from straightforward. His instructions are clear – in their own meandering way. To avoid having your valuables purloined by the local robber, you must follow these directions.

"At each location, you will find a sign telling you how many roads to traverse to get to the next waypoint.

If you find yourself in the mountains, always head north next.

After visiting at a pasture, go south.

From a field, make your way toward the point where the sun sets.

Go east after you enter a forest."

You follow his instructions to the letter and, sure enough, you locate the hills without incident.

Having marked the site, you have only a few hours before sundown. You decided to get home by the fastest route possible.

## What is the shortest route home?

**Solution
p.193**

If you found
the route, add
**1 BRICK**
to your resources

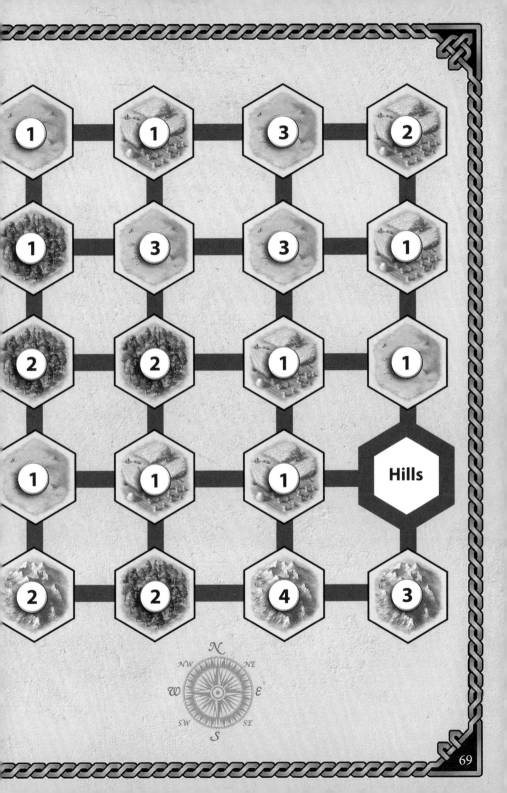

# 35. Please Be Seated

Peaceful co-existence is not something you take for granted. Sometimes, the various groups of workers that comprise your settlement have grievances with one another that can only be resolved at a special gathering of their leaders.

On one occasion, following a particularly heated inter-guild dispute, you call a meeting between the ore miners, brickmakers, woodcutters and shepherds. Each guild sends one representative.

You have chosen a small, intimate hut with just enough space for four chairs and standing room for yourself. Your intention was that no one should feel excluded, but things start to go awry as soon as the delegates arrive.

The ore miner insists on sitting behind the woodcutter and will not sit beside the brickmaker.

The shepherd insists on sitting behind the brickmaker but will not sit beside the woodcutter.

The woodcutter says that if he sits beside the brickmaker, he will only sit behind the ore miner.

**Can you find a way to resolve this seating arrangement using either logic or lateral thinking?**

Solution
p.194

If you fixed the
arrangement, add
**1 ORE**
to your resources

71

# 36. A Road to Bygghofn

There are currently no specialized road builders in your community, so the job falls by necessity to the two guilds whose products are used to construct these vital routes: the woodcutters and brickmakers.

Plans are underway to connect the newly established settlement of Bygghofn to your inland capital, Holmr. You have gathered the best woodcutters and brickmakers to discuss the project and, continuing your budding settlement's time-honoured tradition of working together, both factions proudly offer to do the job single-handedly.

Jora, who leads the woodcutters, says she can build the road in just 27 days. She clearly favours speed over finesse.

Lifa, the brickmaker, offers to build it in 54 days and vows to be more stringent about quality control and safety than her counterpart.

Given that the road is required urgently, and that you want to keep both woodcutters and bricklayers happy, you decree that Jora and Lifa must work together on the project.

## How long will it take to construct the road?

**Solution p.194**

If you calculated the time, add
**1 ROAD**
to your resources

# 37. Short Sharp Shearing

The shepherds and sheep-shearers are a remarkably relaxed group of settlers, content to while away their days on the green pastures in all weathers, while keeping an ever-vigilant eye on their flocks.

They are, however, fiercely competitive at shearing time.

Visiting the annual Fleece Festival, you ask the wise and somewhat mysterious Sigveig the Shepherd how many sheep her sheep-shearers could shear in sheventeen – sorry, seventeen – minutes.

"Seventeen sheep-shearers could shear seventeen sheep in that time," she says.

**Assuming they help each other, how many complete sheep can 45 sheep-shearers shear in three quarters of an hour?**

**Solution p.194**

If you solved the puzzle, add **1 WOOL** to your resources

# 38. Logging II

You are organizing another woodcutting expedition. The forest has been mapped into 64 areas, and the trees that are designated to be cut down are marked with a tree symbol.

Now the woodcutters must be assigned to their trees. You consult the woodcutter's guidebook, known as "The Log", which provides strict rules:

**Distribution of labour:** No more than one woodcutter per tree and the exact number of woodcutters on each row and column must be shown on the diagram.

**Health and safety:** 1. Each woodcutter must stand *beside* their designated tree – that is, in a neighbouring area, horizontally or vertically. 2. No two woodcutters must be *adjacent* to one another – that is, their area must not share a side or corner with another woodcutter's area.

### Can you place the woodcutters by marking their areas with a "W"?

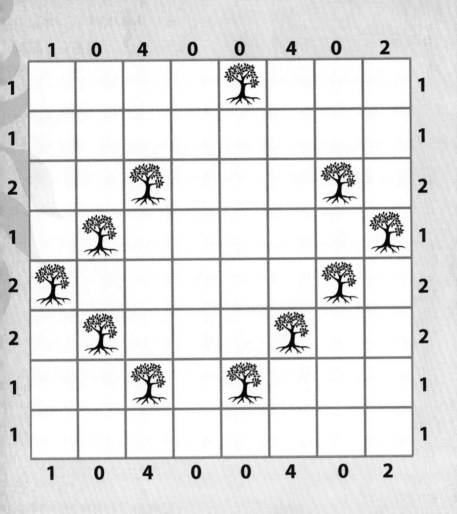

Solution
p.195

If you placed the woodcutters, add **1 LUMBER** to your resources

# 39. Pies for Everyone

The Farmer's Guild make special pastries for the harvest festival and deliver some as a gift to the various worker communities. After loading her cart with 48 freshly baked pies, Marta sets out from her settlement.

First, she visits the shepherds and drops off a dozen mince pies decorated with little pastry sheep.

Then she goes into the woods and delivers a dozen apple pies.

The ore miners similarly receive a dozen Catan pasties.

Finally, Marta heads for the hills, where she is met by 12 hungry brickmakers.

However, the Order of Brickmakers are notorious for their peculiar customs and, according to tradition, Marta must give each brickmaker a loaf, with one left in her basket at the end.

### How can Marta satisfy this tradition?

Solution
p.195

If you solved the puzzle, add
**1 GRAIN**
to your resources

# 40. More Ore

Mining is a dangerous and physically demanding profession, so you can't really blame the Ore Workers' Guild for trying to sell you easily accessible but decidedly sub-standard minerals. However, you can't allow bad product to contaminate the island's nascent economy. You will need to be cunning and diplomatic.

Today, the guild's representative presents you with three carts of ingots. You intend to buy just two of them because you know that one of the carts contains low-grade ingots.

The low-grade ingots each weigh 550 grams, whereas the good quality ingots weigh 500 grams.

Somehow, you have mislaid your perfectly calibrated balance scales, but the representative helpfully offers you the use of his – a more modern design with a weighing basket that can hold up to a dozen ingots and a needle that points to the weight, accurate to the nearest gram.

As always, you must not insult the guild by conducting multiple weighings.

## Can you determine which cart contains the bad ore in just a single weighing?

**Solution p.196**

If you found the correct cart, add **1 ORE** to your resources

# PART 5: DEVELOP

Although your approval among your people is high, some settlers have begun to leave your community to start their own settlement on a recently discovered remote island. You consider their departure ill-advised but their hearts seem set on it, so you don't try to talk them out of leaving.

Months pass and you have received no word from the wayward settlers since they left. Perhaps they have found somewhere better to live, but you cannot shake the feeling that you should have persuaded them to stay…

**"Change does not roll in on the wheels of inevitability but comes through continuous struggle."**

– Martin Luther King Jr.

# 41. Charity

Solutio p.196

If you made it a safely, add
**1 GRAIN**
to your resour

You have finally received a message from some of the settlers who left your community. It is not good news. The island they chose to inhabit has been unyielding, their harvest was poor, and the people are going hungry. With great humility, they ask for your help.

Your own supply of grain and livestock is more than adequate, so you resolve to help them. A gesture of kindness might even repair the rift between your peoples.

However, you feel it would be wise to perform this act of charity quietly, so you decide to go yourself. You are reluctant to travel without any protection whatsoever, so you take your faithful and very energetic wolfhound, Greta, with you.

A cart drops you off at the harbour where your boat is moored. Standing on the shore with Greta, a sack of grain and a sheep, you can immediately see a problem.

The tiny boat can only take one passenger or item at a time, so you must leave the other two on one of the shores.

Greta is no sheepdog; if you leave her alone with the sheep, she's apt to frighten it off, or worse!

Similarly, you cannot leave the sheep alone with the grain. It can chew through the sack and will make short work of such a tasty snack.

## How will you get the grain, the sheep and Greta to the other island to feed the hungry settlers?

# 42. Snow

Winter has come to the island. Snow has fallen during the night and covered the forests, hills, mountains and pastures in a thick white blanket.

The snowfall has been constant across the island. But when lumberjack Torvald meets with his counterpart from the neighbouring settlement, an old logger by the name of Guthrie, he declares, "Your forests have twice as much snow as ours!"

Guthrie acknowledges that this is the case but does not seem too put out.

## Why does Guthrie's forest have so much snow?

Solution
p.196

If you solved the puzzle, add
**1 LUMBER**
to your resources

# 43. Awesome Ore

A variety of metals can be extracted from the island's mountain rocks. Your miners have the arduous and occasionally dangerous job of digging out the ore, which is then processed and crafted into tools and defensive weapons.

In the grid opposite are 15 words relating to (and including) ORE. The words can run horizontally, vertically or diagonally, forwards or backwards.

Here are some clues to help you find the words. The number of letters is in brackets.

1. A metal with something purposefully added (5).
2. Pouring liquid metal into a mould (7).
3. A reddish-brown metal with high conductivity (6).
4. A natural concentration of ore (7).
5. Place for heating and working metals (5).
6. Device for heating metals at high temperatures (7)
7. A metal found in meteorites and blood (4).
8. A malleable, ductile material that conducts heat and electricity (5).
9. Naturally occurring inorganic solid material (7).
10. Naturally occurring solid material from which metals and minerals can be extracted (3).
11. Removal of impurities (8).
12. Glass-like waste left over after metal has been extracted from ore (6).
13. Extraction of metal from ore by heating and melting (8).
14. A craftsman who makes items from metals (5).
15. A sheet-like mass of ore in a fissure (4).

| | | | | | | | | | | | | | | |
|---|---|---|---|---|---|---|---|---|---|---|---|---|---|---|
| H | W | N | N | Q | J | I | N | Q | R | J | P | K | D |
| Z | V | M | I | N | E | R | A | L | J | Q | M | Y | E |
| C | Q | G | S | R | G | O | J | V | L | K | Z | R | P |
| X | C | L | O | Y | X | C | X | M | C | G | H | M | O |
| U | E | Q | A | O | M | J | H | Q | R | D | K | V | S |
| X | N | X | L | R | E | F | I | N | I | N | G | S | I |
| A | P | O | H | F | Z | D | O | O | L | Y | R | C | T |
| C | J | B | N | I | R | V | G | T | Z | E | N | O | A |
| S | M | E | L | T | I | N | G | F | P | F | J | R | E |
| M | E | T | A | L | I | G | F | P | H | W | G | I | R |
| G | N | Z | E | T | Y | D | O | S | X | V | H | A | H |
| U | F | G | S | R | Y | C | L | M | L | E | P | D | C |
| O | R | A | Z | U | N | T | Y | I | B | I | R | O | N |
| O | C | Y | Q | A | D | P | Z | T | W | N | V | G | P |
| Z | M | H | A | L | L | O | Y | H | A | E | L | F | S |

**Solution p.197**

If you found all 15 words, add 1 ORE to your resources

# 44. Ewe Turn

The shepherds Helga and Mimr were once arch-rivals but have since become firm friends. They have divided their sheep so that both shepherds now own a flock of 4 white sheep and 4 black sheep: a total of 16 sheep between them. All of the sheep share a single large pasture. The two shepherds spend their days together, watching their flocks, reminiscing about the silliness of their former feud and giving the other settlers a constant source of idle speculation regarding their relationship.

For the All Settlements Fayre, they have decided to enter just one of their prize white sheep into the competition. It will be the first time they have not competed against one another.

However, on the eve of the fayre, the two shepherds suffer a simultaneous calamity – the gate to the pasture was left open overnight and all the sheep escape!

They immediately fall into a heated argument about whose responsibility it was to lock the gate and harsh words are exchanged.

Just as their disagreement reaches boiling point and both despair of ever seeing their woolly livelihoods again, two of the sheep return home, one belonging to Helga and the other to Mimr.

## What are the chances that one of the sheep is white?

**Solution p.198**

If you calculated correctly, add
**1 WOOL**
to your resources

# 45. Court out

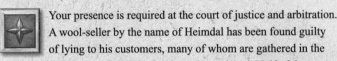 Your presence is required at the court of justice and arbitration. A wool-seller by the name of Heimdal has been found guilty of lying to his customers, many of whom are gathered in the courtroom and calling for him to be severely punished. Half of them demand that he be banished from the community, while the others want his flock to be confiscated.

Either of these punishments would ruin poor Heimdal. In your opinion, he is a shrewd businessman but not a malicious peddler of untruths. You take to the stand and ask the court for clemency, but they will have none of it.

Then you have an idea.

"I shall prove to this court that truth and falsehood are not as clear-cut as you think," you declare. "You say that Heimdal is a liar? Well then, let him condemn himself! Permit him to make a final statement to this court. If his statement is false, let him be banished from our community. If it is true, let his flock be forfeit instead."

A grumble of assent comes from the crowd. They seem satisfied that Heimdal will be ruined one way or another.

As you leave the stand, you give the defendant an encouraging wink and hope his wits are still sharp.

**Solution p.198**

If you saved Heimdal, add 1 WOOL to your resources

## What statement should Heimdal give to the court?

# 46. Natak

You might think that life on the island is nothing but work, but even settlers need recreation from time to time. You have organized feast days and village markets, and encouraged travelling troupes of actors, who bring laughter with them to every settlement they come to.

However, one of the most popular pastimes is natak – a game of skill played by two teams, in which a chunk of brick, wrapped in fleece, is kicked around a field by players in wooden clogs, with the objective of putting it between two iron posts in the other team's half.

The rules, such as they are, make absolutely no sense to anyone who hasn't been stuck on an island for years.

This year, the settlers eagerly await the tournament finals, in which the defending champions, Shepherds United, must win two consecutive games to keep their title.

According to the rules, Shepherds United may choose to face their opponents in any order, provided that they do not play the same team twice in a row. There are two other finalists.

Woodland Wanderers are a stronger team and have won half their games against Shepherds United. Seafarers Select are a weaker team and have never beaten Shepherds United.

## Which order should Shepherds United choose for their three games?

Solution
p.198

If you won the tournament, add
**1 BRICK**
to your resources

1. Woodland   2. Seafarers   3. Woodland

OR

1. Seafarers   2. Woodland   3. Seafarers

# 47. Flocks by Night

Shepherd Helga's flock has expanded considerably since arriving on the island. She now owns 67 sheep: 13 black rams, 24 black ewes, 19 white rams and 11 white ewes.

The formerly rogue island settlement wishes to come back into the fold and has asked for your help in setting up their own pasture. Helga has kindly offered to donate four sheep: a male and a female of each colour. The other colony is sending a boat tonight to collect them.

Unfortunately, it is a pitch-black night and pouring with rain. Consequently, Helga can only herd her sheep by touch, but still needs to have them down by the docks before sunrise.

## How many sheep must Helga take to be sure of having the two pairs that she intends to sell?

**Solution p.198**

If you helped Helga correctly, add **1 WOOL** to your resources

# 48. Ore Processing

Separating ore from rock and high-grade ore from lower-grade minerals is a time-consuming task requiring patience and observation, but it is one of your most valuable resources to trade. Therefore, you decide that you must train only the most diligent to the task. Here is a test that the Ore Workers set for their apprentices.

There are six letters that must be arranged so that each letter only occurs once in each line, in each column and in each 3x2 quadrant.

**Can you fill in the grid and say which six-letter word contained therein would appeal to the ore miners?**

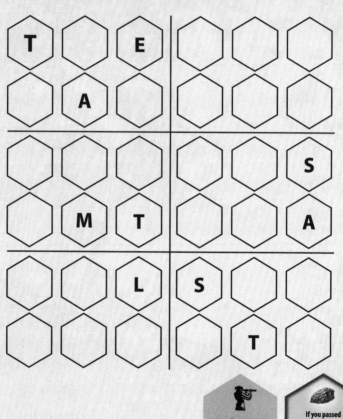

Solution
p.199

If you passed
the test, add
1 ORE
to your resources

# 49. Secret Sequence

The Brickmakers' Guild has an elaborate system of codes that initiates are required to crack before they can become apprentices.

As leader of the community, you expect to be privy to all its secrets, including access to the Brickmakers' Lodge. The master of the guild concurs, provided you can pass the test!

He presents you with this tablet made from unbaked clay and a stylus. "Knowing how things are put together is the essence of brickmaking," he informs you in his heavy baritone. "But not everyone can see what is self-evident. This is the simplest of our tests. Fail and you shall not enter!"

## Which number should you write in the empty space?

| 36 | X | 99 | X | 42 | X | 13 | X | 57 | X | 88 | X | 21 |
|----|---|----|---|----|---|----|---|----|---|----|---|----|

| X | 27 | X | 24 | X | | X | 16 | X | 28 | X | 19 | X |
|---|----|---|----|---|---|---|----|---|----|---|----|---|

**Solution p.199**

If you found the number, add
**1 BRICK**
to your resources

# 50. No Place Like Home

Your settlement contains 100 huts but only 80 per cent are currently occupied. Five percent of the occupied huts contain two settlers each. Of the remaining occupied huts, half house three people each and the others each contain four of your townspeople.

## 1. How many people are there in your community?

Each hut has a door supplied by the woodcutters with a wrought-iron number attached sequentially crafted by the Ore-Workers' Guild.

They construct each numeral in batches but, when they start on the number "9", they find that the ore supplies are running low. The smelters need to know exactly how much ore will be needed to complete the job.

## 2. Can you quickly work out how many number "9"s the smiths will need to craft?

Solution
p.199

If you solved both puzzles correctly, add
1 CITY
to your achievements

# PART 6: EXPAND

You didn't think you could have paradise all to yourself, did you? Other explorers have come to your island and established settlements of their own. Although there are some members of your community who would like to contest our land rights with force, wiser heads have convinced you that the best way forward is peaceful co-existence and profitable trade with the newcomers, meaning attacks on outposts are mercifully extremely rare.

Nevertheless, the issue of "who owns what" is likely to be a thorn in your side for years to come. You will need to be prudent, and clever.

**"Tact is the knack of making a point without making an enemy."**

– Isaac Newton

# 51. Sharing the Land

Four other groups have arrived on one of your islands and staked an equal claim to it. Happily, your diplomatic skills allow you to come to a peaceful solution. The island is to be divided into five regions of different sizes, in which those with a higher concentration of resources will be smaller than those where resources are scarce.

**Can you mentally place the regions opposite so that they fit perfectly onto the island above them, and therefore identify the proposed location of the settlement in each region?**

**Solution
p.198**

If you shared the island fairly, add **1 LUMBER** to your resources

# 52. Changing Tides

The sea is an essential part of island life – both bountiful and hazardous. You take pride in your skills as a sailor and believe your understanding of the ocean to be second to none.

**In the grid below are 15 words relating to (and including) the SEA. The words can run horizontally, vertically or diagonally, forwards or backwards.**

Here are some clues to help you find the words. The number of letters is in brackets.

1. An inward curving coastal inlet (3).
2. The part of land closest to the sea (5).
3. Body of water linking river and sea (7).
4. Aquatic animal with gills and fins (4).
5. Relating to sea life and certain elite soldiers (6).
6. Relating to human activity at sea, such as trade (8).
7. Relating to ships and seafaring (8).
8. Large areas of sea (5).
9. A town or city with access to the sea (4).
10. A submerged ridge of coral, sand or rock (4).
11. Body of saltwater covering 70 per cent of the world's surface (3).
12. Land beside a body of water (5).
13. The rising and falling of the sea due to gravity (4).
14. Dihydrogen monoxide (5).
15. A moving swell of water (4).

**Solution
p.201**

If you found all 15 words, add
**1 LUMBER**
to your resources

| F | O | H | Z | N | A | S | H | O | R | E | C | W | D | M |
|---|---|---|---|---|---|---|---|---|---|---|---|---|---|---|
| O | D | X | V | L | I | L | C | O | U | Q | N | C | Z | A |
| H | J | L | I | X | T | D | G | S | C | U | R | Q | C | R |
| F | K | G | A | I | E | W | D | E | Y | E | Y | Z | Z | I |
| Z | G | K | D | C | Z | S | Z | D | V | M | A | Q | Q | T |
| O | F | E | B | D | I | D | T | I | F | A | B | N | J | I |
| V | E | C | D | Y | F | T | U | U | I | N | W | L | H | M |
| A | J | N | H | U | F | M | U | Z | A | O | X | W | Y | E |
| W | C | X | I | Q | B | L | S | A | W | R | C | Z | K | M |
| R | E | E | F | R | G | X | F | C | N | E | Y | G | K | J |
| P | G | N | O | F | A | F | Q | L | O | T | R | O | P | O |
| B | B | F | C | G | Y | M | X | F | F | A | K | P | Z | S |
| C | O | A | S | T | B | P | F | Q | I | W | U | Q | L | X |
| H | K | C | S | P | E | W | S | T | S | K | Q | E | D | D |
| K | V | E | E | Z | A | D | J | W | H | B | S | E | A | V |

# 53. A Fair Share?

You have recently made contact with the island of Uthrgata, which is a paradigm of inter-community commerce. The island is partitioned into six regions, each under the jurisdiction of an autonomous governor.

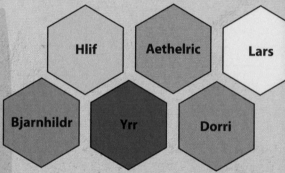

**Hlif**

**Aethelric**

**Lars**

**Bjarnhildr**

**Yrr**

**Dorri**

Each region contains a city and five resource-producing areas.

## 1. Can you fill in the blank areas so that each coloured region, each row and each column contain just one each of the following?

- City
- Brick
- Grain
- Lumber
- Ore
- Wool

**Solutions p.202**

If you solved both puzzles, add **1 GRAIN** to your resources

With large populations living in such close proximity, keeping everyone happy is far from easy. For the cities lucky enough to have coastal access, trade with the outside world provides economic prosperity; for those with landlocked territory, less so.

You can determine the happiness of each region as follows:

For each resource area within a region:

   • add 1 to the region's happiness if the resource area is on the coast.
   • add 1 if the resource area is adjacent (sharing any side, so a central region will share 8 sides, for example) with its own region's city.

For the region's city:

   • add 2 to the region's happiness if it is on the coast.
   • subtract 1 if it is adjacent to another region's city.

## 2. Which governor has the happiest coastal city?

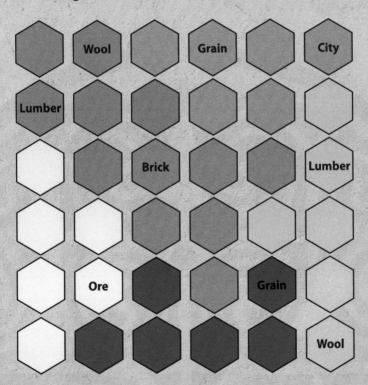

# 54. The Prospector's Provision

One of our community's oldest and most respected settlers has recently passed away: Frigg the Chief Prospector. She will be much missed, both for her remarkable service and her stone-dry wit.

After organizing a funeral fit for such a distinguished member of the community, you find this letter in her cabin:

Dear fellow settlers,

I know a time is soon coming when this island is done with me. I haven't any possessions to speak of, so help yourselves to whatever you can find. Except for you, foreman Jobjorn – you keep your calloused old mitts off of my stuff, you hear?

I've spent the last seven months down in the South Island, trying to make myself useful while my mind and body are still fit for purpose. At 97 years of age, it's not been so easy digging through dirt and fighting off wild dogs.

You may be interested to know that I've flagged up 23 digs. They're numbered on the enclosed map, large enough for even that sorry, short-sighted excuse of a foreman to read.

The veins are a mixed bunch, but only four out of the first nine are really worth a darn. Some of the caves are looking a touch unsafe, but I'm happy to report that the best prospects are also the most secure.

Well, good fortune to you all. Tell that good-for-nothing husband of mine that I expect to see him real soon, when he's done pretending to be a mining foreman.

Frigg the Prospector

**Without even needing to see the map, which one of the numbered sites would you head for first to guarantee finding a good vein of ore?**

Solution
p.203

If you picked the correct site, add
**1 ORE**
to your resources

# 55. Mapmaker

Your scouts bring back reports of another inhabited island. It has an interesting topography – from west to east, there are five distinct regions: hills, woods, mountains, fields and pasture. In each region, there is a northern town and a southern town. Each town is connected to its longitudinal (west–east) neighbour by a single road.

1. The southern town neighbouring the town in the hills is called Farstad.
2. Farstad is three roads away from Gullingen longitudinally.
3. The town called Harmo is directly south of the town called Carlstad.
4. Ennger is directly to the north of the town that is one road from Harmo longitudinally.
5. If Carlstad is not in the northern mountains, then Aarvik is.
6. Dourvik neighbours with Brekke.
7. Brekke is three roads away from Carlstad longitudinally.
8. If Farstad is not in the southern mountains, then Insborg is.
9. Harmo is three roads away from Jorvik longitudinally.
10. Jorvik is not in the southern hills.

**Solution
p.203**

If you located each
town, add
**1 GRAIN**
to your resources

## From the 10 pieces of information provided by your scouts, can you determine the location of each town?

| North | | | | |
|---|---|---|---|---|
| **Hills** | **Woods** | **Mountains** | **Fields** | **Pasture** |
| | | | | |
| South | | | | |

# 56. A Grain of Truth

Visiting other communities always cheers you up. Your settlements might have a few early issues with trade and distribution, but your island neighbours are in a completely different league when it comes to social peculiarities. Your current destination is the curiously named Isle of Truth. According to the island's constitution:

1. Every farmer has sworn to always tell the Truth.
2. The ore miners must protect their interests and will always lie as a matter of principle.
3. Brickmakers must be respected and whatever they say becomes the Truth.

You stay at one of the island's settlements, which has a population of just 18. The settlers have split into three distinct groups of six. You are reliably informed (by a farmer) that one of the groups contains members that all have the same profession, another group is split equally between two professions, and the remaining group is equally split into all three professions.

In the morning, you are introduced to one of the groups and, when you ask their trade, they shout in perfect unison, "We are all farmers!"

That afternoon, you meet the next group, who reply to your question with a harmonious cry of, "We are all ore miners!"

Finally, in the evening, the third group informs you in a loud collective voice, "We are all brickmakers!"

## How many ore miners are there in the community at the end of the day?

Solution
p.204

If you found the right number, add
1 GRAIN
to your resources

**Solution
p.204**

If you made it back
to Sannrborg, add
**1 ORE**
to your resources

# 57. The Way Back

You have been granted a free pass to go wherever you please on the Island
of Truth and decide to take full advantage of this hospitality.

However, sometime after sunset, you realize that you have wandered
far from familiar terrain and onto a winding path that takes you through hill
and vale. You are lost with no clue how to get back to Sannrborg.

Then you stumble upon a pasture where a group of shepherds are
watching their flocks by night. Their names are Nefja, Tofa,
Kjartan and Aeringunnr.

Accepting a very welcome drink, you ask, "Do any of you good folk
know the way to Sannrborg? I'm not sure whether to continue along this path
or turn back."

Nefja replies, "Tofa knows the way to Sannrborg."

Tofa says, "Actually, Aeringunnr can tell you the way."

Kjartan says, "I have no idea where Sannrborg is, sorry."

Aeringunnr says, "Tofa is lying!"

"Only one of them is telling you the Truth – the others are lying ore
miners!"

This last comes from a passing farmer, who then
disappears into the dark forest like a shadow. You know you can trust her, and
consider following her, but don't fancy your chances in the arboreal gloom.
So, it looks like you're stuck with the "shepherds".

## Which of the "shepherds" will you ask for
## directions? And how will you use the information?

# 58. A Busy Week

 You set off to the neighbouring island of Authigr on a trade expedition, with five resources to sell and just one working week to conclude your business. Your itinerary has been drawn up in haste and will require a little logic and judgement to decipher!

**From the clues below, can you work out your week's trading schedule, who you are to meet, where they live, what you are selling them, and where you need to go?**

1. On Monday, you can sell your brick.

2. You can sell your stock of lumber to a trader in the north.

3. Erik will not buy your ore; but you can sell it two days after you see him.

4. You will travel to the west of the island the day before you see Sigrid.

5. On Tuesday, you are heading for the hills.

6. You're looking forward to going south and selling wool in the fields on Friday.

7. In the middle of the week, you are going into the mountains to trade lumber.

8. You can make a sale in the pasture before heading out east the following day.

9. You are meeting Sigrid on the last day of the working week.

10. You are seeing Brigida on Wednesday and Ragnbjorg two days earlier.

11. The woods lie to the west of the island, and you are going there on Thursday.

12. The hills are in the east.

**Location:** Pasture, Hills, Mountain, Woods, Fields

**Traders:** Ragnbjorg, Aestrior, Brigida, Erik, Sigrid

**Days:** Monday, Tuesday, Wednesday, Thursday, Friday

**Resources:** Lumber, Grain, Brick, Ore, Wool

**Directions:** North, South, East, West, Centre

| Day | Mon | Tue | Tue | Wed | Thu | Fri |
|-----------|-----|-----|-----|-----|-----|-----|
| Location  |     |     |     |     |     |     |
| Direction |     |     |     |     |     |     |
| Resource  |     |     |     |     |     |     |
| Trader    |     |     |     |     |     |     |

**Solution p.204**

If you completed your trade trip, add **1 BRICK** to your resources

# 59. Fleeced

The Sauthrs are a family of shepherds and sheep shearers; they are very proud and fiercely competitive.

Every year, they enter the annual sheep-shearing contest. Last year, a team consisting of four of the Sauthr boys sheared 32 fleeces between them and set a new island record.

This year, the theme of the contest is "Ewes and Lambs", so the Sauthrs have sent two mothers along with their respective daughters. They are determined to beat last year's score.

The mothers and daughters are equally skilled and each of them shears exactly 10 sheep – 2 more than the boys' average last year.

However, at the end of the contest, the Sauthr women only have 30 fleeces.

**Can you think of a reason why they didn't beat last year's score?**

**Solution p.205**

If you solved the riddle, add
**1 WOOL**
to your resources

# 60. The Robber

You have convened a court to hear an accusation of sheep rustling.

Helga, the shepherd, has charged a disgruntled settler with stealing one of her precious black ewes. The defendant is a distinctive figure dressed all in black.

Speaking in defence of the potential Robber, his lawyer declares, "As you can see, my client is dressed, as always, in a black robe from head to toe. The sheep in question was also black as pitch."

Addressing Helga, he asks, "Do you possess a working lamp or other means of illumination on your pasture?"

"No, sir," she replies.

"Pitch black and neither torch nor lantern!" intones the lawyer. "How could the shepherd possibly have noticed, let alone identified my client?"

After returning from its deliberations, the jury finds the robber guilty.

## What do you think could have influenced their decision?

Solution
p.205

If you solved the
puzzle, add
1 KNIGHT
to your achievements

# PART 7: TRADE

Many new settlements have been established in neighbouring islands and an era of commerce and prosperity has dawned. Barter is still the preferred type of business transaction and determining the value of things is becoming a popular obsession.

You must ensure that your settlement has access to all the resources it needs to keep one step ahead of your rivals, without losing your reputation as a fair dealer.

**"Peace, commerce and honest friendship with all nations; entangling alliances with none."**

– Thomas Jefferson

# 61. Barter

Although many traders rely on their intuition when assigning value to goods, others prefer a more standardized rate of exchange based on how scarce each resource is.

In Farmathrland, the five resources (brick, grain, lumber, ore and wool) are ranked according to their scarcity. The rarest resource is worth 6, the most common is worth 2, and those in between are worth 3, 4 and 5. This ensures that no trader feels cheated, although it does take away the fun of haggling.

The scarcity ratings are committed to memory, and the only way you can learn what things are worth is by visiting the market and listening to the vendors. So that's what you do.

At his pitch, Oddmarr the ore merchant announces, "I've got two piles of ore for just two bags of grain and three cords of lumber!"

Geira the grain trader shouts, "I've got three bags of grain for two cords of lumber and a reel of wool!"

Warg the wool seller is confused. He tells you that he needs to purchase two stacks of brick and two piles of ore but can't work out the conversion rate.

### How much wool should Warg offer to get what he needs?

**Solution
p.205**

If you calculated
the rates, add
**1 WOOL**
to your resource

# 62. Barter II

In Farmathrland, the five resources are still ranked according to their scarcity, but the values have changed since your last visit, so you'll have to learn them all over again by observation.

The rarest resource is worth 7, the most common is worth 3, and those in between are worth 4, 5 and 6.

You are happy to see that Warg the wool seller is now trading competently: "I can do three reels of wool for one bag of grain and three stacks of brick!" he calls out cheerily.

Geira the grain trader announces, "I've got three bags of grain – yours for just a cord of lumber and a stack of bricks!"

You are looking to purchase some ore, and have brought a cord of lumber, two reels of wool and a stack of bricks to trade with Oddmarr, the ore merchant.

## How much ore can you purchase?

Solution
p.205

If you traded
successfully, add
**1 ORE**
to your resources

# 63. Goods and Services

Trade is the lifeblood of your island society. Through the production and exchange of resources, you have been able to expand your infrastructure and protect the lives and well-being of your settlers. However, some settlers have better access to resources than others and the cracks of social inequality are already starting to show. Will minting coins as a unit of exchange make things better, or worse?

In the grid below are 15 words relating to (and including) TRADE. The words can run horizontally, vertically or diagonally, forwards or backwards.

## Find all 15 words to increase your prosperity!

Here are some clues to help you find the words. The number of letters is in brackets.

1. Exchange goods or services without using money (6).
2. Negotiate terms of a sale; also a great deal (7).
3. To obtain something in exchange for payment (3).
4. Large-scale buying and selling of commodities (8).
5. Participation in the trade of a commodity (4).
6. The state of an area's production and consumption (7).
7. Giving something and receiving something in return (8).
8. Sale and dispatch of goods and services to another country (6).
9. Purchase and receipt of goods and services from another country (6).
10. Coins and notes used as a medium of exchange (5).
11. An area or gathering for the purchase and sale of commodities (6).
12. A person involved in wholesale trade, particularly abroad (8).
13. The exchange value of a thing that can be bought or sold (5).
14. To give something in exchange for payment (4).
15. The action of buying and selling commodities (5).

| | | | | | | | | | | | | | | |
|---|---|---|---|---|---|---|---|---|---|---|---|---|---|---|
| E | X | V | R | P | Q | L | P | N | I | A | G | R | A | B |
| Y | C | K | P | M | F | O | Y | D | J | M | B | H | M | X |
| S | I | M | P | O | R | T | N | T | E | D | A | R | T | N |
| E | D | J | O | L | X | H | M | R | O | A | V | H | I | D |
| X | O | Q | Y | L | Z | F | C | H | K | I | L | B | U | Y |
| C | Y | X | D | J | U | H | O | V | S | J | R | B | X | R |
| H | G | C | F | S | A | J | R | E | X | P | O | R | T | G |
| A | J | R | O | N | Y | Y | L | Y | E | N | O | M | P | D |
| N | D | E | T | M | Z | L | M | O | U | B | L | R | U | Q |
| G | U | T | V | N | M | T | N | O | F | D | I | Z | S | J |
| E | T | R | O | D | V | E | B | I | N | C | W | P | L | K |
| L | U | A | W | A | E | R | R | X | E | O | Z | K | Q | D |
| H | P | B | P | V | G | I | P | C | Y | F | C | E | D | P |
| T | R | K | U | G | L | M | B | O | E | M | Y | E | M | G |
| Y | P | R | O | P | P | N | T | E | K | R | A | M | V | Y |

**Solution p.206**

If you found all 15 words, add **1 LUMBER** to your resources

# 64. A Long Island

You are on a trade expedition to the imaginatively named Langr Island.
The island consists of five regions, each with a unique type of terrain and
a town with an appointed governor. Each town is in need of resources.

**Using the clues below, can you locate the towns
from west to east, ascertain who governs them,
what terrain they enjoy and which resource in what
quantity they require?**

1. Runa is the governor of Hyflinn, a
   town that needs one less resource than
   Fagradal.

2. Magnulf's town needs wool. He doesn't
   much like his neighbour, Thorsen.

3. Thorsen is the governor of the most
   westerly town, which neighbours
   Arendal.

4. Living on the east coast has been good
   for Ljota – her town only needs one
   resource.

5. The town of Reykjar needs brick.

6. The town in the fields needs lumber and
   neighbours the town that only needs
   one resource.

7. Ore is needed in the town of Bjarney,
   which is predominantly pasture.

8. The centre of the island is rolling hills.
   The town situated there is in urgent
   need of grain.

9. Thorsen needs one more resource than
   Ljota.

10. The town in the mountains needs five
    wool.

11. There is a town between the central
    town of Fagradal and the area of
    woods.

12. Birna's town is next to the fields and
    needs four resources.

13. Hyflinn does not neighbour Bjarney.

**Towns:** Arendal, Bjarney, Fagradal, Hyflinn, Reykjar

**Governors:** Birna, Ljota, Magnulf, Runa, Thorsen

**Terrain:** Fields, Hills, Mountains, Pasture, Woods

**Resources needed:** Brick, Grain, Lumber, Ore, Wool

**Quantities:** 1, 2, 3, 4, 5

| | West | | | | East |
|---|---|---|---|---|---|
| Town | | | | | |
| Elder | | | | | |
| Terrain | | | | | |
| Needs | | | | | |
| Quantity | | | | | |

**Solution p.207**

If you completed your trade trip, add **1 GRAIN** to your resources

# 65. Changing Seasons

The Isle of East Langoe is small but rich in resources. Unfortunately, its climate is changing the landscape at an alarming rate. Asfrith, the Weather Sage, has been monitoring the island's topography season by season.

**Which of the options (a, b or c) predicts how the island will look next autumn?**

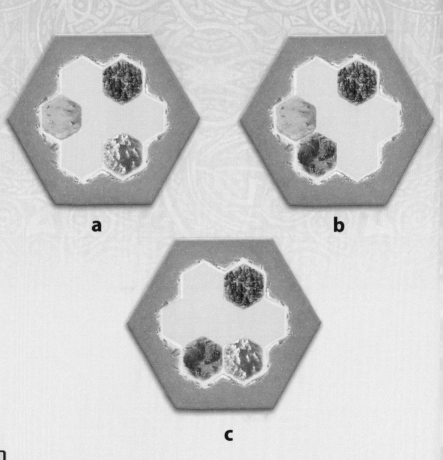

a

b

c

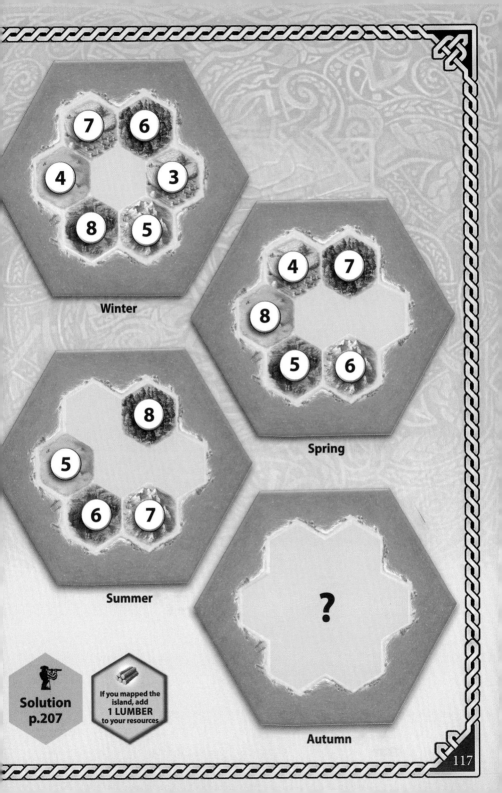

**Winter**

**Spring**

**Summer**

**Autumn**

Solution p.207

If you mapped the island, add **1 LUMBER** to your resources

# 66. Track and Field

Your next road-building project will link up your settlements with grain-producing regions.

## Draw a single continuous line around the grid that passes through all the settlements and fields.

If you enter a settlement, turn left or right within the settlement hexagon and pass straight through the next hexagon you come to. Ensure that this works for both routes going in and out of the settlement.

If you enter a field, keep going straight through the field hexagon and turn left or right in the next hexagon. Ensure that this works for at least one route going into the hexagon.

**Solution
p.207**

If you completed
the road map, add
**1 GRAIN**
to your resources

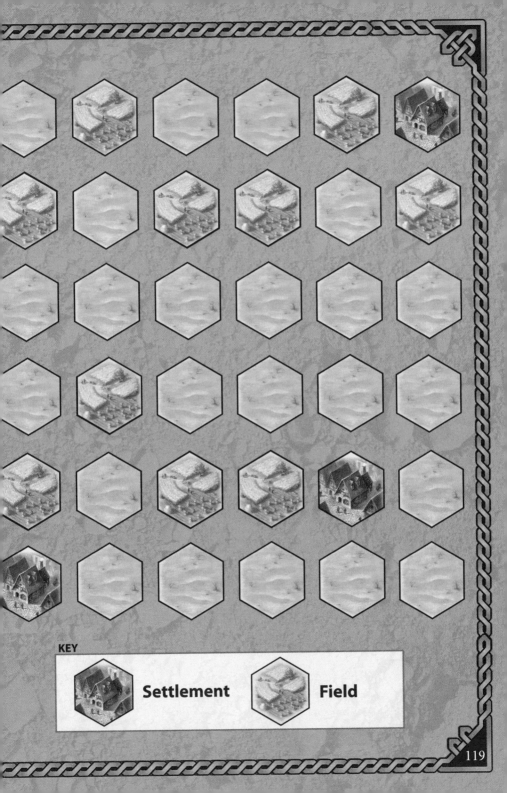

**KEY**

Settlement

Field

# 67. Woolly Warg

Warg the wool seller is expanding his modest business. Not all of his customers are inclined to come to the market at Farmathrland, but the newly constructed island road loop enables him to take his wares to them.

Early one morning, he loads some reels of wool onto his little cart and sets off from Farmathrland.

At noon he arrives at Kongsfjord, where he sells a third of his stock and stops off at the tavern for a jug of refreshing ale.

In the evening, he enters Port Ingen. He sells half of his remaining stock to the local weaver and has a hearty fish supper.

It is almost midnight when he returns to Farmathrland. Being a kind-hearted fellow, he drops one reel off at an elderly neighbour's cottage. The last reel he takes home, and he goes straight to bed. With dreams of wool-earned wealth, he doesn't need to count sheep to fall asleep.

### How many reels of wool did Warg take?

**Solution p.208**

If you calculated correctly, add
**1 WOOL**
to your resources

# 68. Settle the Ore

 After a good day's trading, the merchants Hallstein and Heta prepare to leave the market with identical amounts of ore loaded onto their carts.

Ever competitive, Hallstein can't bear the thought of his trading rival doing as well as him, so he challenges Heta to a game of dice.

Never one to back down from a challenge, Heta agrees.

After seven games, Hallstein finally concedes that luck is not on his side.

"I think you might be a witch!" he says bitterly.

"If I were, I'd turn you into a toad and just take your ore," she retorts with a smirk.

Heta returns home with 28 piles of ore more than Hallstein, which has more than paid for the pair of loaded dice she acquired at the market.

## How much ore did Hallstein lose?

Solution
p.208

If you solved the puzzle, add
**1 ORE**
to your resources

# 69. Coinage

 You are attending the All Communities Trade Fayre, which is held in two settlements: Kaupstathr and Tolsburg. This year, to the chagrin of many settlers, the fayre is trying out some newly minted coins as an alternative to the much-preferred bartering.

At Kaupstathr you hear:
"A bag of grain, a reel of wool and a cord of lumber for just six coins!"
"Two bags and a cord for only four coins!"
"A cord, a stack of bricks and a reel of wool for nine coins!"
"A reel and two stacks for eleven coins!"
"A stack and two bags for six coins!"

The rate of exchange is constant for both buyers and vendors. You must first work out the value of one unit of each resource before you can get down to business.

## 1. You want to buy one unit each of lumber, wool and grain. How many coins will it cost?

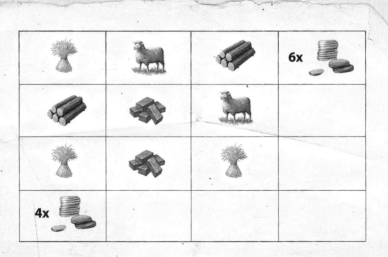

When you get to Tolsburg, you hear a similar cacophony, but find the rate of exchange is different.

"A reel and two piles of ore for eight coins!"
"A cord and two stacks for eleven coins!"
"A stack, a reel and a cord for eight coins!"
"A reel, a pile and a stack for ten coins!"
"A pile, a cord and a stack for nine coins!"

## 2. You want to buy one unit each of ore, wool and brick. How many coins will it cost?

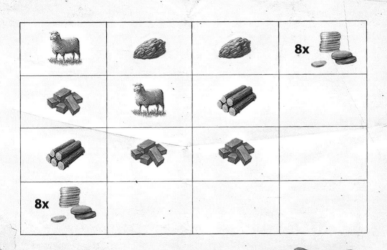

**Solutions p.208**

If you worked out the values, add **1 ROAD** to your resources

# 70. Production Percentage

You have just received word that another island has been discovered, the first new discovery in quite some time. You must decide whether the small island is worth inhabiting or not, but rivals have heard of the discovery. You must make a quick assessment. Every minute counts, and your workers are waiting to do your bidding. Can you calculate the following in under three minutes to determine the island's worth in time?

**1. To the nearest per cent, what percentage of the land of the island contains resource-producing regions?**

**2. What percentage of the producing regions will fall under the brickmaker's jurisdiction?**

**Solution p.208**

If you solved the puzzle in time, add
**1 BRICK**
to your resources

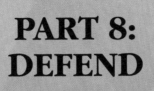

# PART 8: DEFEND

Your settlements are becoming the envy of the inhabited islands, and this is both a blessing and a curse. Since the communities were established, there have been dissident voices from settlers who felt marginalized or were convinced that they were better qualified to govern.

Now that your population has grown, these voices have become factions; individual robbers have become bands of brigands and pirates who threaten the security of your people. You must be ready to defend what you have worked so hard to achieve, or risk losing it all.

**"Igitur qui desiderat pacem, praeparet bellum."**
**(If you want peace, you must prepare for war).**

– Vegetius

# 71. Two Knights Tonight

Just after dusk, two knights ride up to the gates of your settlement. Both have brought lances – long cavalry spears – each exactly 6 feet long.

Three of your guardsmen bar their path and apprise the knights of the settlement's rules. "No horses are permitted inside the settlement after sunset!" bellows the first guard.

"Weapons must be transported inside locked cases!" declares the second guard.

"Cases longer than five-and-a-half feet cannot be brought into the settlement!" states the third.

The two knights nod their understanding and ride on through the gate without dismounting or disarming. The three guards resume their duties without further comment.

## How did the knights enter the settlement unchallenged?

**Solution
p.208**

If you solved the riddle, add
1 ORE
to your resources

# 72. Password

Your spies inform you that the Order of Brickmakers have convened a secret meeting at the behest of Yrsa the Bold, who apparently wants to replace you as the island's next governor.

Not wishing to tip your hand, you make no objection to not being invited but, instead, decide to attend incognito.

Wearing an initiate's hooded robes, you join an orderly queue to enter the Brickmakers' Lodge. But, too late, you realize that there is a password system in place.

The lodge guard ceremoniously bars the way of the brickmaker at the front of the queue and says: "One."

"Three," replies the brickmaker without hesitation.

"Pass, friend!" says the guard, and he steps aside.

The next brickmaker in the queue is challenged.

"Three," says the guard.

"Five" says the guest, and he is permitted to enter.

"Five," says the guard to the person next in line, who is standing in front of you.

"Four," is their reply, and they are ushered through the door.

It is now your turn! Trying to keep your composure and not trip over your oversized robes, you step up to the guard, noting that his huge double-edged battle axe looks anything but ceremonial.

"Four!" he growls.

## What do you do?

**Solution
p.208**

If you made it inside, add
**1 BRICK**
to your resources

# 73. Protect Your People

Robbers and pirates, rebels and wild animals – these are just some of the things that keep you awake at night. Drawing on the wisdom of the Sages, you must devise a defensive system to keep the wilderness at bay.

In the grid below are 15 words relating to (and including) DEFENCE. The words can run horizontally, vertically or diagonally, forwards or backwards.

### Find all 15 words to keep your settlements safe!

Here are some clues to help you find the words. The number of letters is in brackets.

1. Personal protective covering (6).
2. Horse armour (7).
3. Defensive architecture atop castle walls (11).
4. A fortified building with towers and battlements (6).
5. A hinged crossing, raised to protect a castle (10).
6. A military stronghold (8).
7. Armour for your head (6).
8. A device that prevents a door from being opened (4).
9. Water-filled ditch surrounding a castle (4).
10. A defensive wall of stakes (8).
11. Heavy metal grating, lowered to block a gateway (10).
12. A defensive wall around a castle (7).
13. Protection from hostile forces (8).
14. A soldier on guard duty (6).
15. A piece of armour held or strapped to the arm (6).

Solution
p.209

If you found all 15 words, add 1 KNIGHT to your resources

| A | O | A | U | E | L | T | S | A | C | O | H | J | E | H |
|---|---|---|---|---|---|---|---|---|---|---|---|---|---|---|
| T | W | U | X | E | G | D | I | R | B | W | A | R | D | W |
| A | S | H | I | E | L | D | A | H | S | E | N | T | R | Y |
| O | Q | Y | B | Z | Y | M | N | G | D | Q | L | P | V | C |
| M | A | F | T | Y | P | O | J | A | J | P | S | O | B | N |
| M | G | O | L | A | O | P | S | T | H | T | E | R | P | T |
| R | M | R | R | X | P | I | H | E | N | S | C | T | N | Z |
| U | J | T | B | Q | L | C | L | E | C | D | U | C | Y | P |
| O | G | R | P | A | H | M | M | I | N | B | R | U | S | V |
| M | N | E | P | F | E | E | N | G | S | F | I | L | C | Y |
| R | I | S | W | T | L | X | E | L | X | V | T | L | D | Q |
| A | D | S | E | T | N | V | A | O | K | R | Y | I | H | A |
| C | R | I | T | K | D | H | V | C | C | N | S | S | J | G |
| Z | A | A | T | W | G | H | J | K | D | O | I | O | H | R |
| X | B | C | V | O | S | L | U | E | T | V | M | H | S | O |

# 74. Invasion

Not all threats to the island come from pirates and brigands. When the island of Gnogr was first settled, the forested area in the centre was completely stripped of lumber. As you took control, you oversaw a more managed and sustainable use of resources. However, over time the woodland areas have been overrun by ever-expanding pastures and fields, to the detriment of the island's economy.

Looking at the changing face of the island over a three-year period, see if you can discern a pattern.

**If the settlers had not deforested the central area, would it have prevented the pastures and fields from dominating the island?**

Solution
p.210

If you solved the puzzle, add
1 LUMBER
to your resources

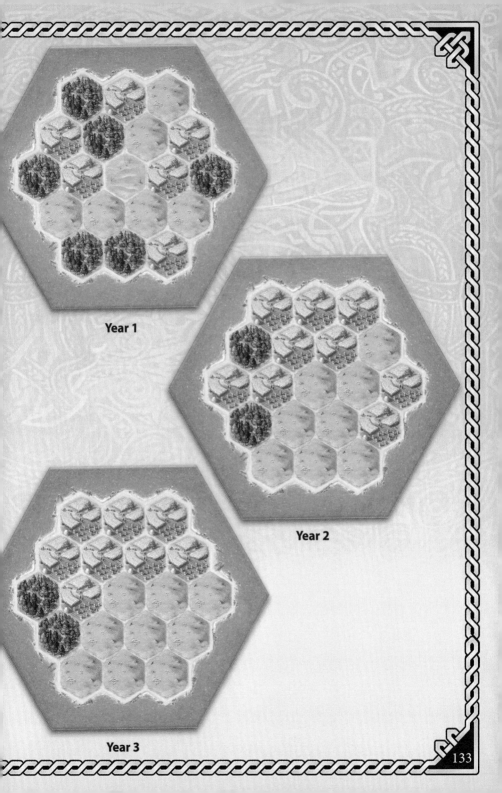

Year 1

Year 2

Year 3

# 75. Taking the Bricks

As part of your ongoing quest to learn the secrets of the Order of Brickmakers, you have been set another challenge by the Sage of the Hills.

He takes you into a candlelit cave, where a hooded neophyte stands before a pile of bricks.

"The Test of Subtraction," intones the sage, "pits neophyte against neophyte. Only one can proceed from here. Behold this stack of freshly baked bricks. You must each take a turn removing one, two or three bricks. The neophyte who takes the last brick shall go no further!"

You quickly count the bricks in the stack. There are 11.

The sage turns to you gravely and says, "You may go first."

## How many bricks should
## you take on your first turn?

**Solution
p.210**

If you worked out
the right number of
bricks, add
**1 BRICK**
to your resources

# 76. Sabotage

The introduction of coinage has not been well received by everyone. A group known as the Master Barter's Guild have been mutteringly suspicious of the new trading practice, but have kept their protests on the right side of the law – until now, it seems.

Three chests of coins are about to be dispatched from the Five Islands' Bank to three different settlements. One chest contains just silver coins and is bound for Authigr, the second contains just copper coins bound for Karlstad, while the third contains a mixture of silver and copper, which is needed in Hogland. Each chest is clearly labelled with its destination.

Or at least they were. During the night, a mischievous troublemaker from the guild switched the labels so that none of the chests had the correct destination attached to it. If the wrong chest is delivered, it could cause an economic and political disaster!

The chests are well-packed, locked and completely tamper-proof. However, your wily spymaster says that it is possible to see a single coin through the keyhole of each chest. You don't have much time before the wagons are supposed to depart.

**Solution
p.211**

**Which chest should you ask the spymaster
to check to determine the correct destinations?**

If you re-labelled
correctly, add
**1 LUMBER**
to your resources

# 77. Protect Your Assets

With your precious resources under constant threat from bands of robbers, you need to build more guard towers!

Opposite is a simplified map of the island, divided into 64 areas, with the vital resource-producing areas highlighted.

The number of towers which must be built on each row and column is shown in the coastal perimeter.

One guard tower – no more, no less – must be built beside each resource area (in a neighbouring area horizontally or vertically).

No two guard towers must be adjacent to one another – that is, their area must not share a side or corner with another guard tower's area.

**Can you determine where the guard towers should be built? One is already placed for you.**

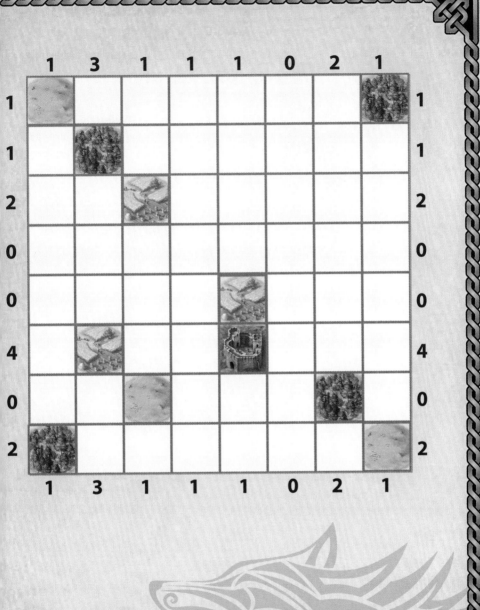

Solution p.211

If you placed the towers, add 1 GRAIN to your resources

# 78. Improvised Security

Robber activity has become prolific around the town of Walda. This might have something to do with the fact that the town's guards are all civilian volunteers with improvised objects for weapons. It appears it is time to hire a more professional set of defenders. Last week, the town lost one of each of its primary resources.

**From the clues below, can you determine who was on guard duty when each resource was stolen, the guard's day job, and the "weapon" they brought to protect the town?**

1. Some grain was stolen while Roskva was on guard duty; she didn't arm herself with either the pickaxe or the rocks.

2. Oddi was armed with a scythe – a fearsome weapon in the right hands, but sadly not his.

3. The miner armed himself with a pickaxe from his workplace; this wasn't Tufi, and neither was it the guard who was on duty when the brick was stolen.

4. The woodworker was not on duty when the ore was stolen.

5. Selbjorn, the shepherd, was not the guard who threw a cabbage in a half-hearted attempt to apprehend the thief who stole the ore.

6. Some lumber was stolen while the farmer was on duty.

**Solution
p.212**

If you solved the puzzle, add
**1 ORE**
to your resources

|  | Shepherd | Miner | Farmer | Woodworker | Brickmaker | Pickaxe | Fishing rod | Rocks | Cabbage | Scythe | Wool | Ore | Grain | Brick | Lumber |
|---|---|---|---|---|---|---|---|---|---|---|---|---|---|---|---|
| Oddi | | | | | | | | | | | | | | | |
| Otama | | | | | | | | | | | | | | | |
| Selbjorn | | | | | | | | | | | | | | | |
| Roskva | | | | | | | | | | | | | | | |
| Tufi | | | | | | | | | | | | | | | |
| Wool | | | | | | | | | | | | | | | |
| Ore | | | | | | | | | | | | | | | |
| Grain | | | | | | | | | | | | | | | |
| Brick | | | | | | | | | | | | | | | |
| Lumber | | | | | | | | | | | | | | | |
| Pickaxe | | | | | | | | | | | | | | | |
| Fishing rod | | | | | | | | | | | | | | | |
| Rocks | | | | | | | | | | | | | | | |
| Cabbage | | | | | | | | | | | | | | | |
| Scythe | | | | | | | | | | | | | | | |

| Settler | Occupation | Weapon | Stolen |
|---|---|---|---|
| Oddi | | | |
| Otama | | | |
| Selbjorn | | | |
| Roskva | | | |
| Tufi | | | |

# 79. The Number

The Order of Brickmakers are very fond of secret codes, but their obsession with numbers means their ciphers are never arbitrary, and this makes them easier to crack.

You notice that members of the inner circle often use numbers as a kind of slang when talking about resources.

"That twelve is only good for torches."

"The weavers are low on eight again."

"Don't accept any low-grade six from those lying tunnel people."

"If the ten fails again this year, we'll starve!"

You find yourself drawn into a conversation with a hooded acolyte and want to ask them about brick. Now would be a good time to show your linguistic credentials and gain their trust.

**What number should you use instead of "brick"?**

**Solution p.212**

If you cracked the code, add
**1 BRICK**
to your resources

# 80. Highways

On a secret visit to the capital of a neighbouring island, you are advised to travel with extreme caution, owing to the number of highwaymen operating in the region. A scout gives you the following instructions:

"At each location, you will find a sign telling you how many roads to traverse to get to the next waypoint.

"After visiting a pasture, head east.

"In the mountains, head west.

"If you find yourself in the woods, go north.

"From a field, you must travel south."

**The capital is your 20th stop. Where did you start your journey?**

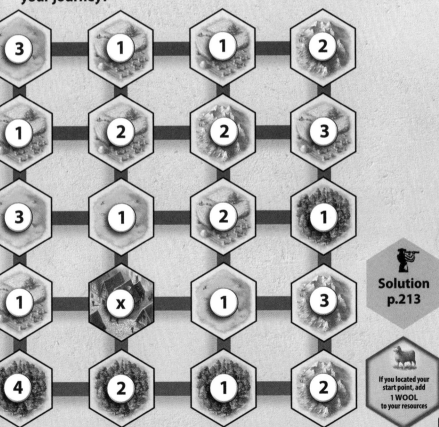

**Solution p.213**

If you located your start point, add **1 WOOL** to your resources

# PART 9: ESTABLISH

From humble beginnings, you have evolved and expanded your settlements into a true island nation. Your people are diverse, and their needs are varied. To govern, you must acknowledge these differences, while being fair in your application of justice.

Leadership can be a thankless task and there are always those who seek to usurp your position. Can you defend it without descending into cynicism, paranoia and tyranny?

**"The heaviest penalty for declining to rule is to be ruled by someone inferior to yourself."**

– Plato

# 81. Another Ship Race

 Your infamous ship race against would-be governor
Magnus the trader is commemorated each year.

Representatives from each of the five guilds compete for
the coveted All Island Trophy by sailing around the mainland.

This year, the favourite to take the trophy is Magnus's daughter,
Yrsa the Bold, who has joined the Order of Brickmakers and seems
every bit as ambitious as her father.

Her ship, the Hydra, is unsurprisingly the most expensive vessel
in the race and reputed to be the fastest thing on the sea.

On the morning of the race, the five racing ships set sail and
receive a tumultuous cheer from the islanders who have gathered
on the coast. As the noonday sun starts to burn, the ships come
back into sight, having circumnavigated the island.

The crowd gasps as the Hydra passes the ship in second place.
But then, to your secret relief, Yrsa's vessel is overtaken by two
ships – belonging to the ore miners and farmers, respectively –
before she reaches the finish line.

**In what place does Yrsa the Bold finish?**

**Solution
p.213**

If you called the race
correctly, add
**1 WOOL**
to your resources

# 82. Team Selection

Seventeen young settlers stand before you, eager to become productive members of the community and join one of the resource-gathering expeditions. The rules of allocation change each year but are very strict. This year, the sages have decreed:

Half the settlers must go to the forest and join the woodworkers.

One third of the settlers must go to the fields and become farmers.

One ninth of the settlers must go to the pasture and work as shepherds.

Clearly, the number of settlers does not fit the fractions, but your community is rather superstitious when it comes to the sages' decrees.

### Can you find a solution?

**Solution
p.213**

If you solved the problem, add
**1 GRAIN**
to your resources

# 83. A Place to Live

 Under wise governance, a small settlement of settlers can grow into a bustling metropolis. The perils of the wilderness may be long forgotten but urban life presents new challenges.

In the grid below are 15 words relating to (and including) the CITY. The words can run horizontally, vertically or diagonally, forwards or backwards.

## Find all 15 words and make yourself at home!

Here are some clues to help you find the words. The number of letters is in brackets.

1. A division of a large town or city (7).
2. Full of activity (8).
3. The city that acts as a region's administrative centre (7).
4. A large, densely populated settlement (4).
5. An urban area comprising of cities and large towns (11).
6. An area of a city with a specific purpose (8).
7. An elected municipal leader (5).
8. A very large city (10).
9. Relating to the government of a town or city (10).
10. An inhabited district (13).
11. Inhabited (9).
12. A long-term inhabitant (8).
13. Unrestricted urban growth (6).
14. Public roads lined with houses and buildings (7).
15. Relating to a town or city (5).

**Solution
p.214**

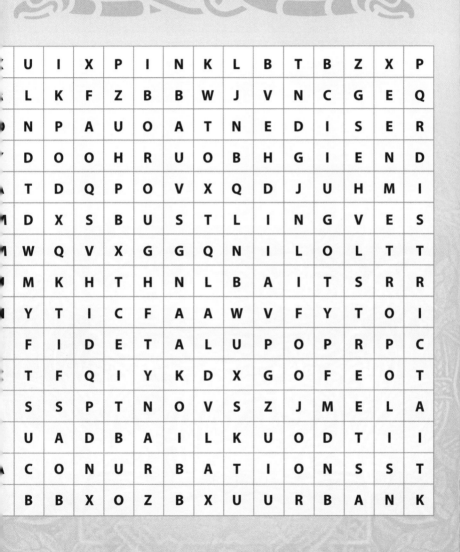

| U | I | X | P | I | N | K | L | B | T | B | Z | X | P |
|---|---|---|---|---|---|---|---|---|---|---|---|---|---|
| L | K | F | Z | B | B | W | J | V | N | C | G | E | Q |
| N | P | A | U | O | A | T | N | E | D | I | S | E | R |
| D | O | O | H | R | U | O | B | H | G | I | E | N | D |
| T | D | Q | P | O | V | X | Q | D | J | U | H | M | I |
| D | X | S | B | U | S | T | L | I | N | G | V | E | S |
| W | Q | V | X | G | G | Q | N | I | L | O | L | T | T |
| M | K | H | T | H | N | L | B | A | I | T | S | R | R |
| Y | T | I | C | F | A | A | W | V | F | Y | T | O | I |
| F | I | D | E | T | A | L | U | P | O | P | R | P | C |
| T | F | Q | I | Y | K | D | X | G | O | F | E | O | T |
| S | S | P | T | N | O | V | S | Z | J | M | E | L | A |
| U | A | D | B | A | I | L | K | U | O | D | T | I | I |
| C | O | N | U | R | B | A | T | I | O | N | S | S | T |
| B | B | X | O | Z | B | X | U | U | R | B | A | N | K |

# 84. Barter and Build

Settlements across the islands are eager to improve the living conditions of their denizens and attract more migration and commerce.

**From the clues below, can you determine what terrain surrounds each settlement, the resource it needs and the building it is hoping to construct?**

1. The name of the settlement that needs ore to build its church is one letter shorter than the settlement in the mountains.

2. Averthen desperately needs more lumber to finish its building project.

3. Robeck is hoping to build a thriving market with the proceeds of its trade.

4. Birkager does not require wool, and neither does the settlement that wants to build a school.

5. Port Flakstad is not building a tavern, and neither is the settlement that requires brick.

6. The settlement in the hills that needs grain does not have the longest or the shortest name.

7. Swilten is surrounded by green pasture.

8. The settlement in the forest is hoping to build a harbour.

**Solution p.215**

If you completed the grid, add
**1 WOOL**
to your resources

|  | Forest | Hills | Pasture | Fields | Mountains | Lumber | Wool | Ore | Grain | Brick | School | Market | Tavern | Church | Harbour |
|---|---|---|---|---|---|---|---|---|---|---|---|---|---|---|---|
| Swilten | | | | | | | | | | | | | | | |
| Port Flakstad | | | | | | | | | | | | | | | |
| Robeck | | | | | | | | | | | | | | | |
| Averthen | | | | | | | | | | | | | | | |
| Birkager | | | | | | | | | | | | | | | |
| School | | | | | | | | | | | | | | | |
| Market | | | | | | | | | | | | | | | |
| Tavern | | | | | | | | | | | | | | | |
| Church | | | | | | | | | | | | | | | |
| Harbour | | | | | | | | | | | | | | | |
| Lumber | | | | | | | | | | | | | | | |
| Wool | | | | | | | | | | | | | | | |
| Ore | | | | | | | | | | | | | | | |
| Grain | | | | | | | | | | | | | | | |
| Brick | | | | | | | | | | | | | | | |

| Settlement | Terrain | Needs | Building |
|---|---|---|---|
| Swilten | | | |
| Port Flakstad | | | |
| Robeck | | | |
| Averthen | | | |
| Birkager | | | |

# 85. Replanting

The island of Askrkorn has used up almost all of its lumber! A major reforestation project is required if it is to have a future.

Forests will be planted in the desert hexes according to the resources produced by their neighbours.

Each hill can be bordered by one forest only.

Each pasture must be bordered by exactly two forests.

Each field must be bordered by exactly three forests.

The city of Port Tre cannot be bordered by any forests – it needs a clear perimeter to protect it from raiders.

**Can you indicate where the forests should be planted?**

**Solution p.215**

If you reforested the island, add **1 LUMBER** to your resources

# 86. Crowns

The ore miners are choosing a new leader for their guild. The ritual of selection is fascinating and steeped in tradition. Five crowns have been specially forged: three of silver and two of gold. The weight of each crown is identical.

The three shortlisted candidates are required to sit blindfolded on three thrones of stone. The crowns are then brought in and the outgoing leader places one on each of the candidate's heads. The two unused crowns are taken from the room and hidden from sight.

In a predetermined order, each candidate removes their blindfold, is given a moment to look at their rivals, and then must state what metal they believe their own crown is made from. If they do not know, each candidate is permitted one "pass". The first candidate to speak true will be the new leader, but if they speak false they are deemed to have failed the test.

It is impossible for a candidate to see their own crown but, according to ore-miner lore, a true Sage of the Mountains can "feel" the difference between gold and silver.

The first candidate removes his blindfold, blinks twice and, after looking at his rivals, says, "I pass."

The second candidate removes her blindfold and, similarly, decides to pass.

The third candidate is perfectly composed and does not even remove their blindfold before correctly guessing the colour of their crown.

**What colour is the third candidate's crown?**

**Solution
p.215**

If you solved the
puzzle, add
1 ORE
to your resources

# 87. Olives

Don Amaro is the governor of a far-off community that has begun trading a new commodity – olives.

The bitter-tasting fruit is already becoming greatly prized on the islands, so you waste no time in assembling a diplomatic team to negotiate a trade deal with Don Amaro.

You arrive at the Don's impressive marble palace, accompanied by wagons packed to bursting with your finest ore, brick, and wool fleeces. However, things start to go downhill when you finally meet the governor.

"We have no need of this… garbage," says the Don dismissively.

The Don's reputation as a rude, deceitful despot is apparently not unfounded.

But then the Don smiles and says, "I'll make you a wager. If you win, I'll trade what you've brought for a wagon of olives. If not, you'll leave your wagons with me and get off my island immediately."

Not a great deal, but you really want those olives.

The Don continues, "I'll put two olives into this bag – a black one and a green one. If you pull out the black one, you win."

One of the Don's servants drops two olives into the bag, but you suspect a trick – you have no doubt that both olives are green.

If you expose the Don's duplicity, you are sure to earn his violent displeasure and will be unlikely to leave the island alive.

## Can you play the Don's game and still win?

**Solution p.216**

If you won the olives, add
**1 LUMBER**
to your resources

# 88. Money

Following the success of the All Communities Trade Fayre, coinage has become all the rage. You visit the markets of Hogland and Gullstathr to purchase resources.

At Hogland, you hear:

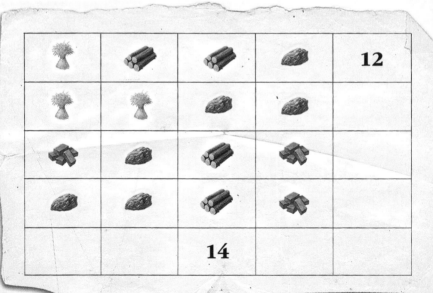

"One bag of grain, two cords of lumber and a pile of ore for twelve coins!"

"Two bags and two piles for twelve coins!"

"Two stacks of bricks, one pile and a cord for thirty coins!"

"Two piles, a cord and a stack for twenty-four coins!"

"A cord, a bag and two piles for fourteen coins!"

"Three cords and a pile for fourteen coins!"

"Two piles and two stacks for thirty-two coins!"

## 1. How much would two bags of grain, a stack of bricks and a pile of ore cost?

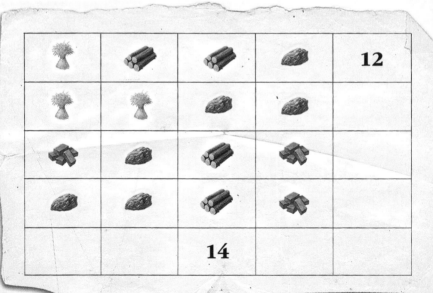

At Gullstathr, you hear:

"Two bags, a cord and a stack for twenty-two coins!"
"A stack, a bag and two reels of wool for twenty-five coins!"
"A bag, a stack, a cord and a reel for twenty-four coins!"
"Three bags and a reel for eighteen coins!"
"A cord, two reels and a stack for twenty-six coins!"
"Two stacks, a reel and a cord for twenty-nine coins!"

## 2. How much for two cords of lumber, a reel of wool and a stack of bricks?

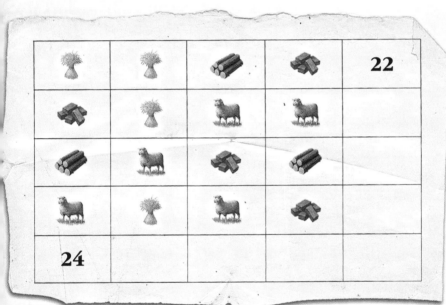

Solutions
p.216

If you struck a
bargain, add
1 ORE
to your resources

# 89. How Many Sheep?

Your community has grown but some things never seem to change. Getting a straight answer out of a group of islanders is always a challenge!

Today, you are trying to track down a couple of sheep-rustling robbers.

You meet three men at a pasture, who introduce themselves as Abjorn, Bekkan and Kjarvald. Very unlikely names, you think. Only one of them can be the honest shepherd. The other two are doubtless local brigands, who are unable to utter a true sentence.

Caution is needed; you must not show your suspicions and tip them off.

Seeing the meadow is devoid of its woolly inhabitants at the moment, you ask how many sheep are currently supposed to be living in the pasture.

"Well, there's definitely more than fifty," says Abjorn.

"Nonsense!" retorts Bekkan. "There are fifty or fewer sheep. No more!"

"Well, there's at least one!" says Kjarvald.

### If only one of the men is telling the truth, who are the brigands and how many sheep live in the pasture?

**Solution p.216**

If you identified the brigands, add **1 KNIGHT** to your achievements

# 90. Ploughshares

Helga has decided to retire from agriculture and invest in ore mining. She announces that she is willing to trade one of her grain fields and a plough for 11 shares in an ore mine.

Petr owns some shares in a mine and is interested in acquiring the field, but he already has a perfectly good plough.

Hoping to persuade him to take the plough off her hands, Helga tells Petr that the field is worth 10 more shares than the plough.

**How many shares must Petr give Helga if he only wants to buy the field?**

**Solution p.216**

If you calculated correctly, add **1 GRAIN** to your resources

# PART 10: ASPIRE

The island nations are bound together by trade treaties, non-aggression pacts and other alliances that have provided years of peace and prosperity. Your people are proud of all that you have achieved and erected a monument in your honour.

Contemplating a comfortable but mundane retirement, your eyes are drawn back to the wide blue ocean. The irresistible desire to explore has taken you once again…

**"Intelligence without ambition is a bird without wings."**

– Salvador Dali

# 91. Year of Plenty

When you settled the Island of Stormenska, Ingrid the farmer converted an area of arable land into a wheat field. The field exactly doubled its yield each year until, in the seventh year, it finally produced enough grain to feed all the inhabitants of the island without any food needing to be imported.

Ingrid has been asked to manage the agriculture on a second island with identical conditions and the same population as Stormenska. She believes she can achieve self-sufficiency for the island in the same time period.

However, the governor would like to speed things up and brings in another farmer, by the name of Lars, who promises he can emulate Ingrid's success.

**If Lars and Ingrid are given a field each, how long would it take them both to provide sustenance for the entire population of the island?**

**Solution p.216**

If you calculate correctly, add
**1 GRAIN**
to your resources

# 92. Bird is the Word

At the market, the vain Yrsa the Bold – who, you are told, is currently plotting to "succeed" you – is intrigued by a brightly coloured bird.

"Is it true that they can talk?" she asks the merchant haughtily.

"Yes, this parrot will repeat any word he hears," he declares.

"How much?"

"To you, six gold pieces."

Yrsa the Bold pays the merchant and seizes the parrot, who lets out an indignant squawk.

A week later, Yrsa returns to the trader in a very sour mood.

"I've been talking to it constantly and this… bird… hasn't uttered a word!" she exclaims.

The parrot takes flight and returns to the merchant with evident relief.

"I want my money back!" she demands. "You mis-sold me the parrot!"

"No, I didn't." says the merchant simply.

**Solution
p.217**

If you absolved the merchant, add
**1 WOOL**
to your resources

## Why is the merchant not guilty of fraud?

# 93. We Need a Hero

As a community grows, it is all too easy for a benevolent government to be transformed by petty rivalries and greed into a despotic bureaucracy. But in such dark times, the example of just one selfless individual can be a beacon of hope.

In the grid below are 15 words relating to (and including) CHIVALRY. The words can run horizontally, vertically or diagonally, forwards or backwards.

## Find all 15 words to bring justice back to your land!

Here are some clues to help you find the words. The number of letters is in brackets.

1. A knight's code of conduct (8).
2. Required to overcome fear (7).
3. Integrity and the respect you earn for having it (6).
4. A knight's four-legged transport (5).
5. Mounted combat at a tournament (8).
6. A noble warrior (6).
7. The spear used by a mounted knight (5).
8. Relating to the Middle Ages (8).
9. Moral excellence and privileged people (8).
10. An exceptional knightly champion (7).
11. The title affixed to a male knight (3).
12. An aspiring knight (6).
13. A long-bladed weapon (5).
14. A sporting competition for knights (10).
15. Someone engaged in armed conflict (7).

Solution
p.217

If you found all
15 words, add
**1 KNIGHT**
to your achievements

| | | | | | | | | | | | | | | |
|---|---|---|---|---|---|---|---|---|---|---|---|---|---|---|
| D | K | R | U | V | T | E | E | D | U | R | O | R | B | E |
| T | Q | I | L | F | C | P | V | S | F | W | I | F | R | X |
| N | Q | U | Y | N | S | Q | A | B | R | S | T | I | F | Q |
| E | W | D | A | W | D | F | I | L | F | O | U | Z | B | H |
| M | R | L | O | L | Z | S | L | S | A | Q | H | R | G | N |
| A | M | R | K | J | W | A | W | X | S | D | C | N | O | L |
| N | D | T | Z | N | V | Z | Y | U | W | V | I | B | B | E |
| R | H | L | B | E | I | R | I | N | E | T | I | N | O | M |
| U | N | X | I | E | L | G | H | X | S | L | W | P | T | G |
| O | V | D | S | A | Q | O | H | U | I | A | Z | J | S | V |
| T | E | J | V | J | N | N | O | T | R | D | M | A | S | M |
| M | V | I | D | O | R | J | Y | R | N | Y | Y | G | E | F |
| P | H | I | U | S | M | B | I | C | O | U | R | A | G | E |
| C | V | R | X | H | W | O | X | Q | N | B | L | R | K | U |
| A | N | S | F | X | R | J | K | W | L | G | O | N | J | P |

# 94. Pastoral Encroachment

Farmers and shepherds often disagree over whether arable land should be used for crops or sheep. The island of Speki has been carefully partitioned to avoid any doubt over ownership, but disagreements often spring up wherever a field shares a long border with a pasture.

**What percentage of Speki's fields share a long border with a pasture?**

Solution
p.218

If you calculated the
percentage, add
**1 GRAIN**
to your resources

# 95. Rescue Mission

You never dreamed that you'd be playing the pirate! But sometimes, the roles of heroes and villains are reversed. No sooner had you stepped down to pass the reins on to the next democratically elected leader, than the cunning Yrsa the Bold seized her chance and took control of the island by force!

"Governor" Yrsa has replaced the town guard with hired bandits and imprisoned the sages! The buildings being used to hold the sages and other loyalists are shown on the map below.

Each building is guarded by a single bandit. If you can determine the position of each bandit, you and your heroic crew of corsairs will be able to free your friends.

The numbers in the perimeter tell you how many bandits are in that row or column.

No two bandits can be adjacent to one another – that is, their area must not share a side or corner with another bandit's area.

**Can you work out where each
bandit is standing?**

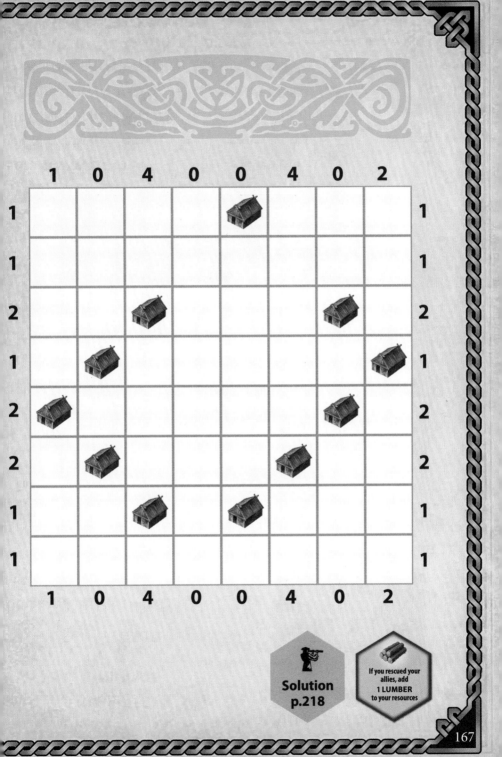

Solution p.218

If you rescued your allies, add 1 LUMBER to your resources

# 96. Expert Advice

Yrsa the Bold is not only a poor governor, but a poor strategist too. With your newly-freed allies by your side, you are sure you can overthrow her and restore your former islands to their true state of peace, freedom and prosperity. You gather three of the island's sages convene a council to discuss the best tactics.

Two of the sages are experts on commerce, two are experts on defence, and two are experts on statecraft. The sage who isn't an expert on statecraft has no understanding of defence. The sage who isn't an expert on defence has no understanding of commerce.

## What are the three sages' areas of expertise?

**Solution p.219**

If you solved the puzzle, add
**1 BRICK**
to your resources

# 97. The Stone of Wisdom

As expected, with your allies at your side and the people's support filling your sails, you overthrow Yrsa the Bold in a bloodless attack – her guards were all too ready to throw down their weapons when they saw you were leading the charge. What's more, the Council of Sages endorses your government. They believe a demonstration of your wisdom might convince your remaining critics that you are every bit as cunning as Yrsa the Bold, and that this will never happen again.

They suggest that you travel to the stone circle on the Isle of Mists and bring back the Stone of Wisdom. Engraved on its surface is a riddle and the key to a code. To unearth it, you must first solve its mystery.

> **Tall in the morning, shorter at noon,**
> **gone when the night falls, but crosses on the moon.**
>
> **+4   +7   +17   +16   -7   +2**
>
> **Shift with the numbers and receive your boon.**

**Can you solve the riddle and decipher the word to prove yourself once more?**

**Solution p.219**

If you solved the riddle, add **1 BRICK** to your resources

# 98. Metropolis

You arrive on your bustling island of Folkvang and notice that it has a transport problem. Its four cities require a continuous road to link them to the resource-producing regions and to one another.

## Draw a single continuous line around the grid that passes through all the cities and resource regions.

If you enter a city, turn left or right within the city's hexagon and pass straight through the next hexagon you come to. Ensure that this works for both routes going in and out of the city.

   If you enter a resource region, keep going straight through its hexagon and turn left or right in the next hexagon. Ensure that this works for at least one route going into the region.

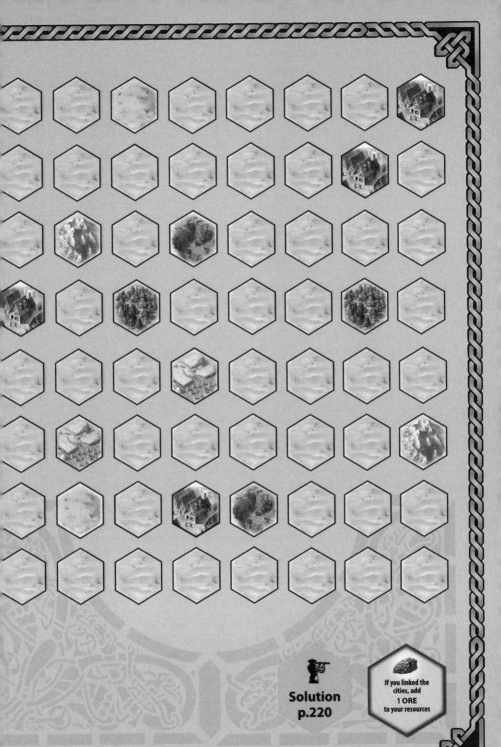

Solution
p.220

If you linked the
cities, add
1 ORE
to your resources

# 99. The Moonwalker Islands

You have encountered a group of islands that have been settled for some time and have well-developed economies. They produce a wide variety of exotic resources that your people have never had access to.

However, trading with the islands is not without risk – each has its own unique hazard.

## From the clues below, can you determine the name of each island's capital city, its particular hazard, and the resource it is trading?

1. The island of Myku has an abundance of exotic spices that are available to trade.
2. The island of Tee-Tow is racked by a civil war; its capital is not Isle Bidair or Kanufleet.
3. The capital city of Aybisi is located on the coast and its trade routes are constantly harassed by pirates. Because of this, its spice route is struggling.
4. Tropical storms are a hazard for the island that trades in silk. This isn't the island of Mallon, whose opulent capital is called Wonchabak.
5. The capital city of Delavu-sayif trades in delicious truffles.
6. Jagki's capital is not Isle Bidair, and Churmayn doesn't trade diamonds. Luckily, neither island's trade is hampered by corrupt officials.
7. Kanufleet is a healthy city and has not had a disease outbreak in living memory.

If you mapped the new islands, add
**1 LUMBER**
to your resources

**Solution**
**p.221**

| | Aybisi | Wonchabak | Isle Bidair | Delavu-sayif | Kunufleet | Corruption | Storms | Pirates | Disease | War | Diamonds | Truffles | Spices | Silk | Rubies |
|---|---|---|---|---|---|---|---|---|---|---|---|---|---|---|---|
| Myku | | | | | | | | | | | | | | | |
| Churmayn | | | | | | | | | | | | | | | |
| Jagki | | | | | | | | | | | | | | | |
| Tee-Tow | | | | | | | | | | | | | | | |
| Mallon | | | | | | | | | | | | | | | |
| Diamonds | | | | | | | | | | | | | | | |
| Truffles | | | | | | | | | | | | | | | |
| Spices | | | | | | | | | | | | | | | |
| Silk | | | | | | | | | | | | | | | |
| Rubies | | | | | | | | | | | | | | | |
| Corruption | | | | | | | | | | | | | | | |
| Storms | | | | | | | | | | | | | | | |
| Pirates | | | | | | | | | | | | | | | |
| Disease | | | | | | | | | | | | | | | |
| War | | | | | | | | | | | | | | | |

| Island | Capital | Hazard | Trading |
|---|---|---|---|
| Myku | | | |
| Churmayn | | | |
| Jagki | | | |
| Tee-Tow | | | |
| Mallon | | | |

# 100.
# The Final Word

And so you come to the end of this chapter in your saga. You have explored the unknown, discovered new lands, and established thriving communities using your gifts of logic and reasoning. The sages themselves are so impressed that they have invited you to a secret meeting.

On Midsummer's Day as the sun rises, you are welcomed into the Grove of Wisdom. Surrounded by ancient standing stones and the wisest minds on the island, you are given a final riddle that will prove whether you are worthy to join the Academy of Sages.

The oldest of the sages intones:

"Starting with a word of just one letter, add a letter to create a new word. Keep adding a letter and creating a new word until you reach an eight-letter word that takes you back to the beginning."

## What is the final word?

**Solution
p.221**

If you solved
the riddle, add
**1 CITY**
to your achievements

# SOLUTIONS

# 1. Landfall

**B.** Each hexagon is formed of six types of terrain (triangles) that "point" either due east or west. Each type of triangle within a hexagon must point in the opposite direction to the same type in neighbouring hexagons.

If you completed the map, add
**1 SETTLEMENT**
to your achievements

# 2. First Impressions

| Scout | Direction | Time | Resource |
|---------|-----------|---------|----------|
| Morgana | North | Morning | Lumber |
| Frigg | Centre | Evening | Ore |
| Bjorn | South | Noon | Brick |

If you solved the puzzle, add
**1 LUMBER**
to your resources

# 3. Agriculture

1. Barley
2. Bran
3. Cereal
4. Corn
5. Crop
6. Cultivate
7. Flour
8. Germ
9. Grain
10. Harvest
11. Kernel
12. Oat
13. Mill
14. Sow
15. Wheat

If you found all 15 words, add **1 GRAIN** to your resources

| C | L | T | L | V | Z | B | D | C | C | O | G | G | C | S |
|---|---|---|---|---|---|---|---|---|---|---|---|---|---|---|
| L | G | C | L | W | L | W | L | O | C | D | Q | E | S | P |
| U | X | R | Q | M | I | I | E | R | H | S | K | C | R | H |
| V | B | O | S | J | N | B | D | N | T | N | D | V | F | M |
| Z | L | P | S | D | S | P | T | E | X | M | L | G | R | L |
| V | T | V | W | W | D | O | T | U | K | I | R | U | E | H |
| H | H | S | M | X | E | A | W | P | Z | L | O | N | Q | A |
| X | Y | G | P | T | V | D | W | B | L | L | R | D | B | R |
| J | Y | Z | R | I | L | S | U | T | F | E | M | M | O | V |
| W | X | A | T | A | B | A | W | B | K | V | T | F | A | E |
| Y | H | L | G | J | I | P | J | A | G | W | H | E | U | S |
| F | U | E | R | H | F | N | Q | R | G | B | U | C | V | T |
| C | N | X | A | Y | J | B | K | L | J | F | R | Q | J | O |
| T | T | M | C | T | C | E | R | E | A | L | S | A | H | A |
| Y | C | G | X | I | B | U | C | Y | U | C | J | H | N | T |

# 4. The Merry Lumberjacks

Arranging the statements in a more orderly fashion helps to determine which are mutually exclusive.

Agnar:
"I cut down eighteen trees." **(FALSE)**
"I cut down four fewer than Ingeborg."
"I cut down two more trees than Jarl."

Ingeborg:
"I did not cut down the fewest trees."
"The difference between the trees I cut down and the number that Jarl cut down was six."
"Jarl cut down twenty-four trees." **(FALSE)**

Jarl:
"I chopped down fewer trees than Agnar."
"Agnar cut down twenty trees."
"Ingeborg cut down six more trees than Agnar." **(FALSE)**

So Agnar cut down 20 trees, Ingeborg cut down 24 trees and Jarl cut down 18 trees.

If you discovered the
truth, add
**1 LUMBER**
to your resources

# 5. Neighbourhood

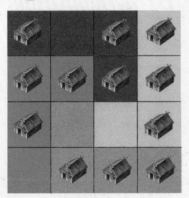

If you solved the puzzle, add **1 WOOL** to your resources

# 6. Svart Mountain

**Yes.** Imagine that there was another ore prospector making the return journey (at the faster pace) on the day that Frigg set out – at some point, the two would have to meet.

If you solved the puzzle, add **1 ORE** to your resources

# 7. The Ship Race

**"Swap ships!"** After your amendment, you are not only the better sailor, but you are sailing the faster ship as well. As long as you win the race, which is almost a certainty now, the ship that you own will come in last.

If you won the race, add **1 WOOL** to your resources from Magnus's stores

# 8. Pyramid Scheme

**15 moves.**

| | |
|---|---|
| 1 | Smallest to B |
| 2 | Small to C |
| 3 | Smallest to C |
| 4 | Large to B |
| 5 | Smallest to A |
| 6 | Small to B |
| 7 | Smallest to B |
| 8 | Largest to C |
| 9 | Smallest to C |
| 10 | Small to A |
| 11 | Smallest to A |
| 12 | Large to C |
| 13 | Smallest to B |
| 14 | Small to C |
| 15 | Smallest to C |

If you moved the bricks correctly, add
**1 BRICK**
to your resources

# 9. Guard Duty

**Half past four in the morning**. It takes you 17-and-a-half minutes to get to the first post, you stand at a post for a total of 6 hours and there are 11 changes taking a total of 55 minutes, plus the journey home makes 7-and-a-half hours.

If you solved the puzzle, add
**1 BRICK**
to your resources

# 10. Mathematical Certainty

**Because it makes a difference!**

If you solved the riddle, add
**1 GRAIN**
to your resources

# 11. Island Hopping

**E.** On each island, the centre hexagon contains all six resource triangles except one key resource, which is replaced by desert. The key resource rotates clockwise in the five hexagons surrounding the centre of each island, swapping its position with the succeeding triangle.

If you completed the map, add
**1 ORE**
to your resources

# 12. Into the Woods

1. Branch
2. Carpenter
3. Forestry
4. Logging
5. Lumberjack
6. Maple
7. Oak
8. Pine
9. Plank
10. Sawmill
11. Stick
12. Timber
13. Tree
14. Trunk
15. Wood

If you found
all 15 words, add
**1 LUMBER**
to your resources

| T | G | X | B | N | D | P | P | Y | Q | H | E | N | H | P |
|---|---|---|---|---|---|---|---|---|---|---|---|---|---|---|
| U | R | I | R | O | Z | L | O | G | G | I | N | G | H | Q |
| B | U | U | O | M | T | A | T | P | K | X | M | O | A | K |
| J | N | W | N | L | U | M | B | E | R | J | A | C | K | K |
| F | J | F | X | K | C | H | D | X | S | M | H | K | H | I |
| M | F | D | Y | C | X | N | Q | G | A | A | N | G | Q | R |
| S | P | R | B | T | O | L | B | D | V | D | X | Z | E | T |
| A | L | I | B | R | A | N | C | H | N | X | Y | T | C | I |
| W | A | B | N | E | F | Z | M | R | F | Q | N | M | E | M |
| M | N | M | G | E | S | K | V | U | K | E | K | B | X | B |
| I | K | A | S | X | A | W | M | O | P | U | N | Z | R | E |
| L | R | P | H | T | Z | F | O | R | E | S | T | R | Y | R |
| L | U | L | W | B | I | O | A | R | C | T | E | B | C | W |
| L | L | E | W | L | V | C | R | T | S | N | F | D | K | W |
| H | T | W | U | X | T | D | K | L | F | W | K | F | T | E |

# 13. Out for the Count

The settlement has **28 sheep** (each with 4 legs) and **44 shepherds** (with 2 legs each). You should perhaps turn your attention to fixing this imbalanced ratio.

If you deciphered the note, add
**1 WOOL**
to your resources

# 14. The First Harvest

Let x be the number of hectares in each field. Sigge cleared three hectares of wheat, and the entire barley field except for six hectares. He therefore cleared x-3 hectares. Steinn, on the other hand, cleared x+3 hectares, and so receives the **most ingots by six.**

If you solved the puzzle, add
**1 GRAIN**
to your resources

# 15. Island Index

**9.** The sage first added the values of ore plus brick, and wool plus grain together. He then found the product of those two numbers, before subtracting the values of the wood and water consumed.

$(5+5) \times (5+5) - (5+5) =$ **90**
$(3+4) \times (4+5) - (1+2) =$ **60**
$(7+2) \times (3+3) - (4+6) =$ **44**
$(1+9) \times (8+2) - (7+3) =$ **90**

If you found the value, add
**1 BRICK**
to your resources

# 16. Road Loop

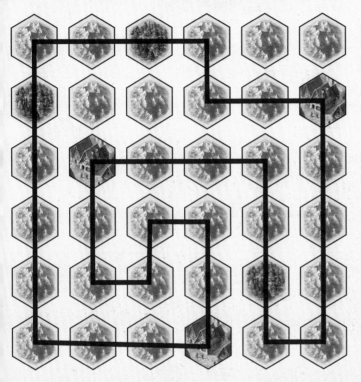

# 17. The Island
# in the Island

If Ragna ties the rope to the tree on the shore and walks
around the island, it will wrap itself around the oak and
create a sturdy double line. Using her formidable athletic
skills and the pole for balance, she should be able to get to
the island and plant a flag.

# 18. Mist Directions

Put the signpost back into the ground with the "Harbour" arrow pointing back the way you came.

If you found your way, add **1 WOOL** to your resources

# 19. Obscurity

**Region 24** contains hills from where you can obtain brick. If you are struggling, regions 1 and 3 are forests. See if you can fill the rest from there.

If you identified the region, add **1 LUMBER** to your resources

# 20. The Following Day

| Resource | Workers | Problem | Leader |
|---|---|---|---|
| Brick | 10 workers | Landslide | Egil |
| Ore | 12 workers | Wild dogs | Jarnsaxa |
| Lumber | 15 workers | Fire | Fenrir |

If you solved the puzzle, add **1 ORE** to your resources

# 21. Stronger Foundations

If you solved the puzzle, add **1 BRICK** to your resources

The total is **25 bricks.** The resource level is equal to the number of hexes with that resource level. Hence, there is one "1", two "2"s, three "3"s, etc. The missing numbers are 7 and 5.

# 22. Baa!

1. Bleat
2. Ewe
3. Fleece
4. Flock
5. Knitting
6. Lamb
7. Mutton
8. Pasture
9. Ram
10. Shearing
11. Sheep
12. Shepherd
13. Spinning
14. Wool
15. Yarn

If you found all 15 words, add **1 WOOL** to your resources

| V | Q | P | C | F | L | E | E | C | E | N | X | J | W | K |
| S | L | N | F | L | J | F | N | O | B | C | I | P | Y | X |
| H | U | O | F | O | I | M | I | G | D | C | K | Q | P | M |
| E | C | J | Q | C | U | H | G | Y | D | X | Y | A | A | U |
| A | L | R | K | K | K | N | I | T | T | I | N | G | S | T |
| R | S | M | U | K | I | B | O | W | Q | A | C | W | T | T |
| I | Y | I | Q | N | J | F | E | T | A | X | U | B | U | O |
| N | M | P | N | Q | M | H | A | L | F | A | V | J | R | N |
| G | W | I | Z | Q | Z | E | P | K | L | A | I | M | E | D |
| V | P | Z | G | T | L | E | O | C | F | T | W | S | L | M |
| S | N | P | N | B | E | Y | P | K | X | X | Y | O | L | H |
| S | O | I | H | H | E | P | A | X | K | E | O | I | L | I |
| P | X | G | S | B | F | K | V | R | U | W | N | Z | A | O |
| M | I | R | Z | L | K | R | A | M | N | E | S | H | M | W |
| J | Z | M | V | U | S | H | E | P | H | E | R | D | B | S |

# 23. Job Creation

| Name | Quality | Job |
| --- | --- | --- |
| Alfbjorn | Boisterous | Woodcutter |
| Baldr | Honest | Shepherd |
| Caecilia | Fastidious | Brickmaker |
| Dagmaer | Patient | Farmer |
| Eric | Strong | Miner |

If you assigned the jobs correctly, add **1 SETTLEMENT** to your achievements

# 24. Multi-Tasking

Oda: brickmaking, defence, harvesting, shepherding

Gudmund: defence, harvesting, ore mining, woodcutting

Skjald: brickmaking, ore mining, shepherding, woodcutting

If you found your way, add **1 GRAIN** to your resources

# 25. Black and White

**"At least half are ewes"** and **"Over a third are ewes"** are technically true statements, even if **ALL the flock are ewes.** It looks like you'll need to buy some rams if you want your wool production to continue for years to come.

If you discovered the problem, add **1 WOOL** to your resources

# 26. What's in a Name?

First, let's establish the facts:

- **Sven cannot be the farmer.**
- **Yrsa cannot be the miner.**
- **Alfrikr cannot be the shepherd.**
- **Nal cannot be the woodcutter.**

Now look at the locals' statements:

The first statement (that Sven is the woodcutter) cannot be true if the third statement (that Yrsa is not the woodcutter, Sven is) is false. They must therefore both be false, so either the second or fourth are true. If the fourth was, Nal would be a shepherd and ultimately Yrsa would be a farmer, meaning the third speaker had told a partial truth. Only if the second statement is true, are all three others wholly false:

- **Sven is the shepherd.**
- **Yrsa is the woodcutter.**
- **Alfrikr is the farmer.**
- **Nal is the miner.**

If you identified
the liars, add
**1 GRAIN**
to your resources

# 27. Mining Community

From the remaining 189 settlers, we can see that 49 are in poor health. If we subtract that number from the number of hard workers (70), we are left with 21. Subtracting the number of children gives 10, and if we then subtract the 8 settlers who refuse to work as miners, we are left with a worst-case scenario of just **2 miners.**

If you solved the
puzzle, add
**1 ORE**
to your resources

# 28. Ore, or...

Put three ingots on one side of the scales and three ingots on the other. If one side is heavier than the other, the ingots on that side become the "suspects" in the second weighing.

However, if the first six ingots balance, the three ingots that you have not yet weighed are the "suspects".

Put one of the "suspect" ingots on each side of the scales. If one is heavier, it is the fake. However, if they balance, the remaining un-weighed "suspect" ingot is the fake.

If you found
the fake ingot, add
**1 ORE**
to your resources

# 29. The Apprentices' Test

 You should have chiselled the **blue symbol.** The two lower bricks always determine which brick should lay on top of them, as follows:

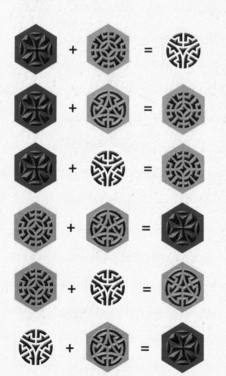

If you passed the
test, add
**1 BRICK**
to your resources

If you placed the woodcutters, add **1 LUMBER** to your resources

# 30. Logging

| 0 | 3 | 0 | 3 | 0 | 2 | 2 | 2 | |
|---|---|---|---|---|---|---|---|---|
|   | W | 🌳 | W |   | 🌳 | W |   | 3 |
|   |   |   | 🌳 |   |   |   | 🌳 | 0 |
|   |   |   | W | 🌳 | W |   | W | 3 |
| 🌳 | W |   | 🌳 |   |   |   |   | 1 |
|   |   |   |   |   |   | W | 🌳 | 1 |
|   |   | 🌳 | W |   |   |   |   | 1 |
|   | 🌳 |   |   |   |   | 🌳 | W | 1 |
|   | W |   |   | 🌳 | W |   |   | 2 |
| 0 | 3 | 0 | 3 | 0 | 2 | 2 | 2 | |

# 31. New Islanders

Sven might be the oldest sibling, but only by minutes.
**The children are triplets!**

If you solved the riddle, add **1 GRAIN** to your resources

# 32. Woodcraft

The carpenter is building a **coffin.**

If you solved the riddle, add **1 LUMBER** to your resources

# 33. Building Blocks

1. Block
2. Bond
3. Bricklayer
4. Clay
5. Construction
6. Course
7. Frog
8. Header
9. Kiln
10. Masonry
11. Mortar
12. Quoin
13. Road
14. Stretcher
15. Wall

If you found all 15 words, add **1 BRICK** to your resources

| M | V | F | Y | A | X | W | U | R | X | D | N | V | P | Y |
|---|---|---|---|---|---|---|---|---|---|---|---|---|---|---|
| M | Q | U | O | I | N | S | E | B | L | G | B | W | N | R |
| W | X | C | A | G | X | D | B | F | I | M | J | A | L | Q |
| P | B | O | C | U | A | D | J | R | O | A | D | L | N | X |
| V | O | N | N | E | Y | Z | W | O | N | Y | Y | L | S | B |
| L | N | S | H | W | C | J | Q | G | A | O | V | I | G | R |
| A | D | T | Q | W | W | K | B | L | O | C | K | R | J | I |
| C | I | R | K | I | L | N | C | M | C | Y | M | R | R | C |
| M | E | U | F | U | S | D | H | C | M | O | Q | Z | Q | K |
| A | M | C | B | Z | L | J | V | A | R | F | U | L | E | L |
| S | U | T | N | U | F | I | G | A | L | S | C | R | Z | A |
| O | S | I | P | X | R | S | T | F | X | E | C | P | S | Y |
| N | S | O | E | P | X | R | N | D | K | F | K | K | D | E |
| R | A | N | D | B | O | R | W | P | H | H | S | Y | V | R |
| Y | P | I | K | M | S | T | R | E | T | C | H | E | R | U |

# 34. The Brick Road

You must travel **three roads due north** to get home.

If you found
the route, add
**1 BRICK**
to your resources

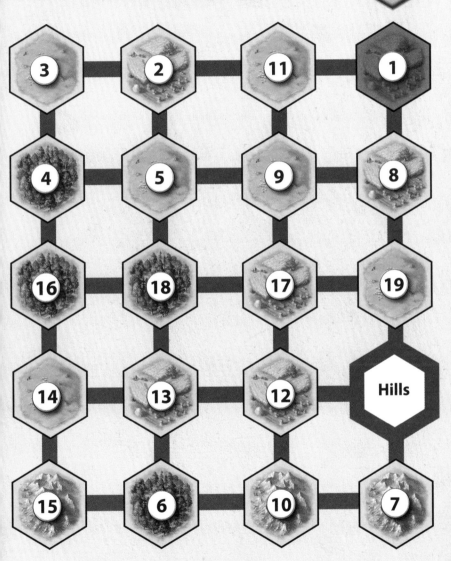

# 35. Please Be Seated

**Turn the rear chairs so that they are facing in the opposite direction,** so that the ore miner and the woodcutter are effectively behind one another, as are the shepherd and the brickmaker.

If you fixed the arrangement, add **1 ORE** to your resources

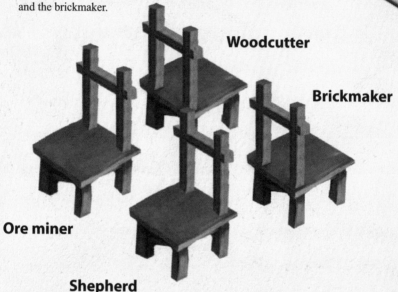

**Woodcutter**

**Brickmaker**

**Ore miner**

**Shepherd**

# 36. A Road to Bygghofn

In a single day, Lifa completes $^1/_{54}$ of the road while Jora completes $^2/_{54}$, for a total of $^3/_{54}$. Dividing 54 by 3 gives you the answer: **18 days.**

If you calculated the time, add **1 ROAD** to your resources

# 37. Short Sharp Shearing

They could shear **119 sheep.** One shearer can shear one sheep in 17 minutes, so they can shear $^1/_{17}$ sheep in one minute. Forty-five can therefore shear $^{45}/_{17}$ in one minute, or $^{2025}/_{17}$, or 119.1 sheep, in 45 minutes.

If you solved the puzzle, add **1 WOOL** to your resources

# 38. Logging II

If you placed the woodcutters, add **1 LUMBER** to your resources

|   | 1 | 0 | 4 | 0 | 0 | 4 | 0 | 2 |   |
|---|---|---|---|---|---|---|---|---|---|
| 1 |   |   |   |   | 🌳 | W |   |   | 1 |
| 1 |   |   | W |   |   |   |   |   | 1 |
| 2 |   |   | 🌳 |   |   | W | 🌳 | W | 2 |
| 1 |   | 🌳 | W |   |   |   |   | 🌳 | 1 |
| 2 | 🌳 |   |   |   |   | W | 🌳 | W | 2 |
| 2 | W | 🌳 | W |   |   | 🌳 |   |   | 2 |
| 1 |   |   | 🌳 |   | 🌳 | W |   |   | 1 |
| 1 |   |   | W |   |   |   |   |   | 1 |
|   | 1 | 0 | 4 | 0 | 0 | 4 | 0 | 2 |   |

# 39. Pies for Everyone

Marta hands out 11 loaves and gives the basket containing the last loaf to the 12th brickmaker.

If you solved the puzzle, add **1 GRAIN** to your resources

195

# 40. More Ore

**Yes, you can.** Take one ingot from the first cart, two ingots from the second and three from the third. If the first cart contains bad ingots, the basket will weigh 3,050 grams; if they are in the second cart, it will weigh 3,100 grams; and if they are in the third, it will weigh 3,150 grams.

If you found
the correct cart, add
**1 ORE**
to your resources

# 41. Charity

1. Take the sheep to the other island, leaving Greta on your home island with the grain.
2. Leave the sheep on the other island, then return to your island.
3. Bring Greta over to the other island, leave her there and return home with the sheep.
4. Leave the sheep on your island and take the grain over to the other island.
5. Finally, go back to your island alone, pick up the sheep and set off once more to the other island.

If you made it across
safely, add
**1 GRAIN**
to your resources

# 42. Snow

Guthrie's forest is **twice the size** of Torvald's.

If you solved the
puzzle, add
**1 LUMBER**
to your resources

# 43. Awesome Ore

Alloy
Casting
Copper
Deposit
Forge
Furnace
Iron
Metal

9. Mineral
10. Ore
11. Refining
12. Scoria
13. Smelting
14. Smith
15. Vein

If you found all 15 words, add **1 ORE** to your resources

| I | H | W | N | N | Q | J | I | N | Q | R | J | P | K | D |
| I | Z | V | M | I | N | E | R | A | L | J | Q | M | Y | E |
| X | C | Q | G | S | R | G | O | J | V | L | K | Z | R | P |
| F | X | C | L | O | Y | X | C | X | M | C | G | H | M | O |
| U | U | E | Q | A | O | M | J | H | Q | R | D | K | V | S |
| R | X | N | X | L | R | E | F | I | N | I | N | G | S | I |
| N | A | P | O | H | F | Z | D | O | O | L | Y | R | C | T |
| A | C | J | B | N | I | R | V | G | T | Z | E | N | O | A |
| C | S | M | E | L | T | I | N | G | F | P | F | J | R | E |
| E | M | E | T | A | L | I | G | F | P | H | W | G | I | R |
| I | G | N | Z | E | T | Y | D | O | S | X | V | H | A | H |
| Y | U | F | G | S | R | Y | C | L | M | L | E | P | D | C |
| V | O | R | A | Z | U | N | T | Y | I | B | I | R | O | N |
| U | O | C | Y | Q | A | D | P | Z | T | W | N | V | G | P |
| F | Z | M | H | A | L | L | O | Y | H | A | E | L | F | S |

# 44. Ewe Turn

There are four equally likely possibilities:

1. Both sheep are white.
2. Both are black.
3. Helga's is white and Mimr's is black.
4. Mimr's is white and Helga's is black.

So the chances of one being white is **three in four.**

If you calculated
correctly, add
1 WOOL
to your resources

# 45. Court Out

Heimdal declares, **"I shall be banished from the community."** If this statement is taken as true, he should lose his flock, but that would then render the statement false. If the statement is taken as false, he should be banished, which would immediately render it true. It is a paradox, which fortunately gave the court pause for thought and encouraged a gentler sentence for Heimdal.

If you saved
Heimdal, add
1 WOOL
to your resources

# 46. Natak

Remember that United must win two consecutive games. So, although it might be tempting to face Seafarers twice, the **first is the best option.** Since United are almost guaranteed to win the middle game against Seafarers, this gives them two opportunities to beat Woodland (a three-in-four chance of winning one game and the tournament). In the second option, everything hinges on the second game, which they have a 50-50 chance of winning.

If you won the
tournament, add
1 BRICK
to your resources

# 47. Flocks by Night

Helga must take **57 sheep!** The worst case would be all 24 of the black ewes, all 19 white rams, all 13 black rams and one of the white ewes.

If you helped Helga
correctly, add
1 WOOL
to your resources

# 48. Ore Processing

**The word is METALS.**

If you passed
the test, add
**1 ORE**
to your resources

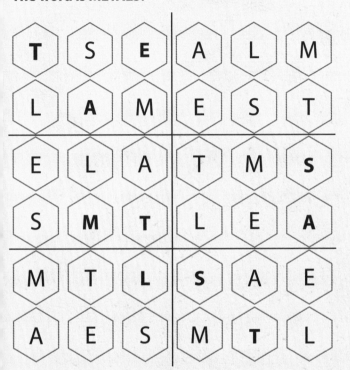

# 49. Secret Sequence

**The missing number is 10.** Add the individual digits of the top two numbers together to get the value of the bottom number that lies between them.

If you found the
number, add
**1 BRICK**
to your resources

# 50. No Place Like Home

**1. 274 settlers** (20x0 + 4x2 + 38x3 + 38x4).
**2. 20.**

If you solved both
puzzles correctly, add
**1 CITY**
to your achievements

# 51. Sharing the Land

If you shared the
island fairly, add
**1 LUMBER**
to your resources

# 52. Changing Tides

1. Bay
2. Coast
3. Estuary
4. Fish
5. Marine
6. Maritime
7. Nautical
8. Ocean
9. Port
10. Reef
11. Sea
12. Shore
13. Tide
14. Water
15. Wave

If you found all 15 words, add **1 LUMBER** to your resources

| F | O | H | Z | N | A | S | H | O | R | E | C | W | D | M |
| O | D | X | V | L | I | L | C | O | U | Q | N | C | Z | A |
| H | J | L | I | X | T | D | G | S | C | U | R | Q | C | R |
| F | K | G | A | I | E | W | D | E | Y | E | Y | Z | Z | I |
| Z | G | K | D | C | Z | S | Z | D | V | M | A | Q | Q | T |
| O | F | E | B | D | I | D | T | I | F | A | B | N | J | I |
| V | E | C | D | Y | F | T | U | U | I | N | W | L | H | M |
| A | J | N | H | U | F | M | U | Z | A | O | X | W | Y | E |
| W | C | X | I | Q | B | L | S | A | W | R | C | Z | K | M |
| R | E | E | F | R | G | X | F | C | N | E | Y | G | K | J |
| P | G | N | O | F | A | F | Q | L | O | T | R | O | P | O |
| B | B | F | C | G | Y | M | X | F | F | A | K | P | Z | S |
| C | O | A | S | T | B | P | F | Q | I | W | U | Q | L | X |
| H | K | C | S | P | E | W | S | T | S | K | Q | E | D | D |
| K | V | E | E | Z | A | D | J | W | H | B | S | E | A | V |

# 53. A Fair Share?

1.

If you solved both puzzles, add **1 GRAIN** to your resources

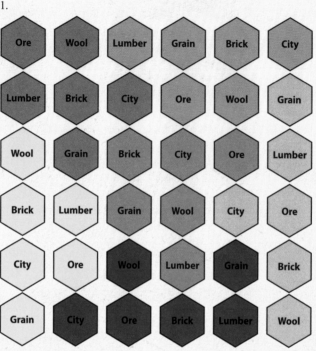

2. **Lars** has the happiest city.

|  | Brick | Grain | Lumber | Ore | Wool | City | Points |
|---|---|---|---|---|---|---|---|
| **1 Aethelric** | 2 | 1 | 1 | 0 | 1 | 2 | 7 |
| **2 Bjarnhildr** | 1 | 1 | 1 | 1 | 2 | -1 | 5 |
| **3 Dorri** | 1 | 1 | 0 | 1 | 1 | -2 | 2 |
| **4 Hlif** | 2 | 1 | 2 | 2 | 1 | -1 | 7 |
| **5 Lars** | 2 | 2 | 1 | 1 | 1 | 1 | 8 |
| **6 Yrr** | 1 | 0 | 1 | 2 | 1 | 1 | 6 |

# 54. The Prospector's Provision

**Vein number nine** would be your best bet. Frigg would have written "four out of the first eight" if it were not so.

# 55. Mapmaker

| North | | | | |
|---|---|---|---|---|
| Carlstad | Ennger | Aarvik | Brekke | Dourvik |
| **Hills** | **Woods** | **Mountains** | **Fields** | **Pasture** |
| Harmo | Farstad | Insborg | Jorvik | Gullingen |
| South | | | | |

1. Clue 1 = Farstad in the south woods.
2. Clue 2 = Gullingen in the south pasture.
3. Clue 8 = Insborg in the south mountains.
4. Clue 10 = Jorvik in the south fields.
5. Clue 9 = Harmo in the south hills.
6. Clue 3 = Carlstad in the north hills.
7. Clue 4 = Ennger in the north woods.
8. Clue 5 = Aarvik in the north mountains.
9. Clue 7 = Brekke in the north fields.
10. Clue 6 = Dourvik in the north pasture.

If you found the correct site, add **1 ORE** to your resources

If you located each town, add **1 GRAIN** to your resources

# 56. A Grain of Truth

A farmer could never claim to be an ore miner (they can't lie) and an ore miner could never admit to being an ore miner (they can't tell the truth).

Therefore, the group declaring itself to be all ore miners must be all brickmakers, who now become ore miners in accordance with the constitution (+ 6 ore miners).

Given that the group with all 3 professions must contain some truth-telling farmers, it has to be the first group you met. This group must also contain 2 bricklayers (who are transformed into farmers) and 2 lying ore miners (+ 2 ore miners).

The group that declared itself to be all brickmakers consists of 2 professions: three brickmakers and three lying ore miners (+ 3 ore miners).

So, by the end of the day, there are **11 ore miners** in the community, including the former brickmakers.

If you found the right number, add
**1 GRAIN**
to your resources

# 57. The Way Back

The only person who can be telling the truth is Aeringunnr, which means **Kjartan** knows the way. As Kjartan has proven to be a compulsive liar, you should go in the opposite direction to the one he gives you.

If you made it back to Sannrborg, add
**1 ORE**
to your resources

# 58. A Busy Week

| Day | Mon | Tue | Wed | Thu | Fri |
|-----------|-----------|-------|-----------|----------|--------|
| Location | Pasture | Hills | Mountains | Woods | Fields |
| Direction | Centre | East | North | West | South |
| Resource | Brick | Grain | Lumber | Ore | Wool |
| Trader | Ragnbjorg | Erik | Brigida | Aestrior | Sigrid |

If you completed your trade trip, add
**1 BRICK**
to your resources

# 59. Fleeced

The Sauthrs only sent three shearers, across three generations: a grandmother and her daughter, who was the mother of the third sheep shearer.

If you solved the riddle, add
**1 WOOL**
to your resources

# 60. The Robber

The robbery occurred **during the daytime!**

If you solved the puzzle, add
**1 KNIGHT**
to your achievements

# 61. Barter

The scarcity ratings are:

| Lumber | Grain | Brick | Wool | Ore |
|--------|-------|-------|------|-----|
| 2 | 3 | 4 | 5 | 6 |

So Warg should offer **four reels of wool.**

If you calculated the rates, add
**1 WOOL**
to your resources

# 62. Barter II

The scarcity values are:

| Grain | Lumber | Brick | Wool | Ore |
|-------|--------|-------|------|-----|
| 3 | 4 | 5 | 6 | 7 |

So you can purchase **three piles of ore.**

If you traded successfully, add
**1 ORE**
to your resources

# 63. Goods and Services

1. Barter
2. Bargain
3. Buy
4. Commerce
5. Deal
6. Economy
7. Exchange
8. Export
9. Import
10. Money
11. Market
12. Merchant
13. Price
14. Sell
15. Trade

If you found all 15 words, add **1 LUMBER** to your resources

| E | X | V | R | P | Q | L | P | N | I | A | G | R | A | B |
| Y | C | K | P | M | F | O | Y | D | J | M | B | H | M | X |
| S | I | M | P | O | R | T | N | T | E | D | A | R | T | N |
| E | D | J | O | L | X | H | M | R | O | A | V | H | I | D |
| X | O | Q | Y | L | Z | F | C | H | K | I | L | B | U | Y |
| C | Y | X | D | J | U | H | O | V | S | J | R | B | X | R |
| H | G | C | F | S | A | J | R | E | X | P | O | R | T | G |
| A | J | R | O | N | Y | Y | L | Y | E | N | O | M | P | D |
| N | D | E | T | M | Z | L | M | O | U | B | L | R | U | Q |
| G | U | T | V | N | M | T | N | O | F | D | I | Z | S | J |
| E | T | R | O | D | V | E | B | I | N | C | W | P | L | K |
| L | U | A | W | A | E | R | R | X | E | O | Z | K | Q | D |
| H | P | B | P | V | G | I | P | C | Y | F | C | E | D | P |
| T | R | K | U | G | L | M | B | O | E | M | Y | E | M | G |
| Y | P | R | O | P | P | N | T | E | K | R | A | M | V | Y |

# 64. A Long Island

| | West | | | | East |
|---|---|---|---|---|---|
| **Town** | Bjarney | Arendal | Fagradal | Hyflinn | Reykjar |
| **Elder** | Thorsen | Magnulf | Birna | Runa | Ljota |
| **Terrain** | Pasture | Mountains | Hills | Fields | Woods |
| **Needs** | Ore | Wool | Grain | Lumber | Brick |
| **Quantity** | 2 | 5 | 4 | 3 | 1 |

If you completed your trade trip, add
**1 GRAIN**
to your resources

# 65. Changing Seasons

**C.** The lowest numbered region becomes a desert and the remaining numbers cycle clockwise through the non-desert regions.

If you mapped the island, add
**1 LUMBER**
to your resources

# 66. Track and Field

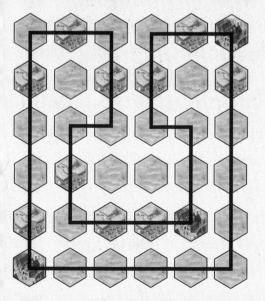

If you completed the road map, add
**1 GRAIN**
to your resources

# 67. Woolly Warg

**Six.** He sold two reels at Kongsfjord and two at Port Ingen, taking two back to Farmathrland.

If you calculated correctly, add
**1 WOOL**
to your resources

# 68. Settle the Ore

Hallstein lost all **14 piles** of his ore.

If you solved the puzzle, add
**1 ORE**
to your resources

# 69. Coinage

### 1. Kaupstathr
It would cost **6 coins.**

1 bag of grain costs 1 coin.
1 cord of lumber costs 2 coins.
1 reel of wool costs 3 coins.
1 stack of bricks costs 4 coins.

### 2. Tolsburg
It would cost **10 coins.**

1 cord of lumber costs 1 coin.
1 reel of wool costs 2 coins.
1 pile of ore costs 3 coins.
1 stack of bricks costs 5 coins.

If you worked out the values, add
**1 ROAD**
to your resources

# 70. Production Percentage

1. **35 per cent** of the island is productive.

2. The brickmakers will own **25 per cent** of the resource-producing regions.

If you solved the puzzle in time, add
**1 BRICK**
to your resources

# 71. Two Knights Tonight

The knights were riding on a wagon pulled by oxen. They had also complied with the rule requiring weapons to be stored in locked cases. Their lance cases measured 5 feet by 4 feet, allowing their 6-foot lances to be placed inside diagonally.

If you solved the riddle, add
**1 ORE**
to your resources

# 72. Password

Keep your cool and say **"four"**. The correct response is the number of letters in the number given by the guard.

If you made it inside, add
**1 BRICK**
to your resources

# 73. Protect Your People

1. Armour
2. Barding
3. Battlements
4. Castle
5. Drawbridge
6. Fortress
7. Helmet
8. Lock
9. Moat
10. Palisade
11. Portcullis
12. Rampart
13. Security
14. Sentry
15. Shield

If you found all 15 words, add **1 KNIGHT** to your resources

| A | O | A | U | E | L | T | S | A | C | O | H | J | E | H |
|---|---|---|---|---|---|---|---|---|---|---|---|---|---|---|
| T | W | U | X | E | G | D | I | R | B | W | A | R | D | W |
| A | S | H | I | E | L | D | A | H | S | E | N | T | R | Y |
| O | Q | Y | B | Z | Y | M | N | G | D | Q | L | P | V | C |
| M | A | F | T | Y | P | O | J | A | J | P | S | O | B | N |
| M | G | O | L | A | O | P | S | T | H | T | E | R | P | T |
| R | M | R | R | X | P | I | H | E | N | S | C | T | N | Z |
| U | J | T | B | Q | L | C | L | E | C | D | U | C | Y | P |
| O | G | R | P | A | H | M | M | I | N | B | R | U | S | V |
| M | N | E | P | F | E | E | N | G | S | F | I | L | C | Y |
| R | I | S | W | T | L | X | E | L | X | V | T | L | D | Q |
| A | D | S | E | T | N | V | A | O | K | R | Y | I | H | A |
| C | R | I | T | K | D | H | V | C | C | N | S | S | J | G |
| Z | A | A | T | W | G | H | J | K | D | O | I | O | H | R |
| X | B | C | V | O | S | L | U | E | T | V | M | H | S | O |

# 74. Invasion

**No**, it would only have delayed the spread very briefly. Each year, a hex that is bordered by more of one type of terrain than another changes to that terrain type.

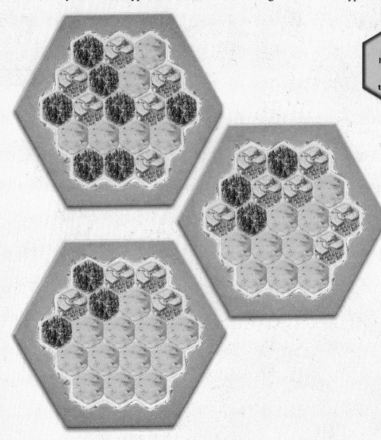

If you solved the puzzle, add **1 LUMBER** to your resources

# 75. Taking the Bricks

You should take **two bricks.** Your objective is to take the sixth brick, which will guarantee victory. With five remaining, no matter how many your opponent takes on their turn, you can then take a number which will leave them with the last brick. By taking two initially, you can guarantee taking the sixth brick.

If you worked out the right number of bricks add **1 BRICK** to your resources

# 76. Sabotage

Check the chest labelled **"Hogland"**, which is supposed to contain silver and copper coins. Since you know it is incorrectly labelled, if the spymaster sees a copper coin, the chest must contain all copper and, therefore, be intended for Karlstad. If she sees a silver coin, the chest should be be relabelled "Authigr". Swap the "Hogland" label with the other labelled chest, and put that chest's label on the third chest.

If you re-labelled correctly, add **1 LUMBER** to your resources

# 77. Protect Your Assets

If you placed the towers, add **1 GRAIN** to your resources

|   | 1 | 3 | 1 | 1 | 1 | 0 | 2 | 1 |   |
|---|---|---|---|---|---|---|---|---|---|
| **1** | | | | | | | | | **1** |
| **1** | | | | | | | | | **1** |
| **2** | | | | | | | | | **2** |
| **0** | | | | | | | | | **0** |
| **0** | | | | | | | | | **0** |
| **4** | | | | | | | | | **4** |
| **0** | | | | | | | | | **0** |
| **2** | | | | | | | | | **2** |
|   | 1 | 3 | 1 | 1 | 1 | 0 | 2 | 1 |   |

211

# 78. Improvised Security

| Settler | Occupation | Weapon | Stolen |
|---------|------------|--------|--------|
| Oddi | Farmer | Scythe | Lumber |
| Otama | Miner | Pickaxe | Wool |
| Selbjorn | Shepherd | Rocks | Brick |
| Roskva | Woodworker | Fishing rod | Grain |
| Tufi | Brickmaker | Cabbage | Ore |

# 79. The Number

If you solved the puzzle, add
**1 ORE**
to your resources

**"Five".** The number is derived from the number of vowels in the word, multiplied by its length.

Lumber = twelve
Wool = eight
Ore = six
Grain = ten
Brick = five

If you cracked the code, add
**1 BRICK**
to your resources

# 80. Highways

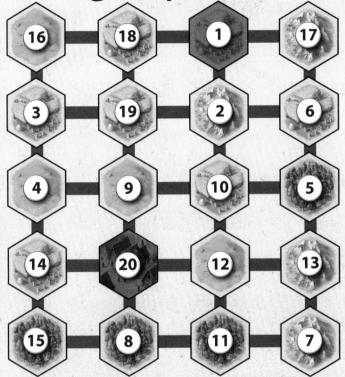

If you located your start point, add
**1 WOOL**
to your resources

# 81. Another Ship Race

**In fourth place.** If the answer was obvious, congratulations on your concrete reasoning or visualization. Many wrongly assume that overtaking the ship in second place would put her in the lead, rather than taking the second-place slot.

If you called the race correctly, add
**1 WOOL**
to your resources

# 82. Team Selection

**Volunteer yourself!** You are a settler after all. This will bring the total number of workers to 18. Therefore, nine join the woodworkers, six join the farmers and two join the shepherds. That accounts for all 17 of the young settlers, and you won't have to get your own hands dirty!

If you solved the problem, add
**1 GRAIN**
to your resources

# 83. A Place to Live

1. Borough
2. Bustling
3. Capital
4. City
5. Conurbation
6. District
7. Mayor
8. Metropolis
9. Municipal
10. Neighbourhood
11. Populated
12. Resident
13. Sprawl
14. Streets
15. Urban

If you found all 15 words, add **1 BRICK** to your resources

| X | U | I | X | P | I | N | K | L | B | T | B | Z | X | P |
|---|---|---|---|---|---|---|---|---|---|---|---|---|---|---|
| R | L | K | F | Z | B | B | W | J | V | N | C | G | E | Q |
| O | N | P | A | U | O | A | T | N | E | D | I | S | E | R |
| Y | D | O | O | H | R | U | O | B | H | G | I | E | N | D |
| A | T | D | Q | P | O | V | X | Q | D | J | U | H | M | I |
| M | D | X | S | B | U | S | T | L | I | N | G | V | E | S |
| M | W | Q | V | X | G | G | Q | N | I | L | O | L | T | T |
| U | M | K | H | T | H | N | L | B | A | I | T | S | R | R |
| N | Y | T | I | C | F | A | A | W | V | F | Y | T | O | I |
| I | F | I | D | E | T | A | L | U | P | O | P | R | P | C |
| C | T | F | Q | I | Y | K | D | X | G | O | F | E | O | T |
| I | S | S | P | T | N | O | V | S | Z | J | M | E | L | A |
| P | U | A | D | B | A | I | L | K | U | O | D | T | I | I |
| A | C | O | N | U | R | B | A | T | I | O | N | S | S | T |
| L | B | B | X | O | Z | B | X | U | U | R | B | A | N | K |

# 84. Barter and Build

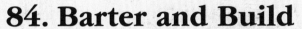

If you completed the grid, add
**1 WOOL**
to your resources

| Settler | Terrain | Needs | Building |
|---------|---------|-------|----------|
| Swilten | Pasture | Ore | Church |
| Port Flakstad | Forest | Wool | Harbour |
| Robeck | Fields | Brick | Market |
| Averthen | Mountains | Lumber | School |
| Birkager | Hills | Grain | Tavern |

# 85. Replanting

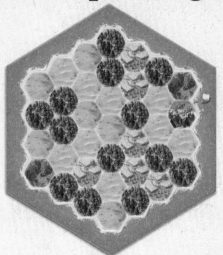

If you reforested the island, add
**1 LUMBER**
to your resources

# 86. Crowns

**Silver.** The first candidate could have only been sure of his own crown's colour if the other two were wearing gold crowns. Knowing that at least one of the crowns is silver, the second candidate could only answer certainly if the first candidate's crown was gold. As she passed, her rivals must both be wearing silver crowns – giving the third candidate the answer without any need to check.

If you solved the puzzle, add
**1 ORE**
to your resources

# 87. Olives

Take an olive from the bag without letting anyone see its colour and **put it straight into your mouth!** Spit out the pip, congratulating the Don on the quality of his olives and state that the only way to know the colour of the olive you just ate is to pull the other olive from the bag.

If you won the olives, add **1 LUMBER** to your resources

# 88. Money

### 1. Hogland

It would cost 18 coins.
1 bag of grain costs 1 coin.
1 cord of lumber costs 3 coins.
1 pile of ore costs 5 coins.
1 stack of bricks costs 11 coins.

### 2. Gullstathr

It would cost 25 coins.
1 bag of grain costs 4 coins.
1 cord of lumber costs 5 coins.
1 reel of wool costs 6 coins.
1 stack of bricks costs 9 coins.

If you struck a bargain, add **1 ORE** to your resources

# 89. How Many Sheep?

**Abjorn and Kjarvald must be the brigands.** If there is one or more sheep, then Kjarvald and another "shepherd" must both be telling the truth. Therefore, there must be **no sheep**, and Bekkan is telling the truth.

If you identified the brigands, add **1 KNIGHT** to your resources

# 90. Ploughshares

We know that:
1 field + 1 plough = 11 shares,
and 1 field = 10 shares + 1 plough

So…
10 shares + 2 ploughs = 11 shares
2 ploughs = 1 share
1 plough = ½ a share

If you calculated correctly, add **1 GRAIN** to your resources

Therefore, **the field is worth 10 ½ shares.**

# 91. Year of Plenty

Assuming Lars lives up to his word, it would take **six years.** In year six, Ingrid's farm alone will be halfway toward its target, so two farms would produce the required amount of grain.

If you calculated correctly, add **1 GRAIN** to your resources

# 92. Bird is the Word

The parrot will repeat any word that he hears, but sadly **the parrot is deaf.**

If you absolved the merchant, add
**1 WOOL**
to your resources

# 93. We Need a Hero

1. Chivalry
2. Courage
3. Honour
4. Horse
5. Jousting
6. Knight
7. Lance
8. Medieval
9. Nobility
10. Paladin
11. Sir
12. Squire
13. Sword
14. Tournament
15. Warrior

If you found all 15 words, add
**1 KNIGHT**
to your resources

| D | K | R | U | V | T | E | E | D | U | R | O | R | B | E |
|---|---|---|---|---|---|---|---|---|---|---|---|---|---|---|
| T | Q | I | L | F | C | P | V | S | F | W | I | F | R | X |
| N | Q | U | Y | N | S | Q | A | B | R | S | T | I | F | Q |
| E | W | D | A | W | D | F | I | L | F | O | U | Z | B | H |
| M | R | L | O | L | Z | S | L | S | A | Q | H | R | G | N |
| A | M | R | K | J | W | A | W | X | S | D | C | N | O | L |
| N | D | T | Z | N | V | Z | Y | U | W | V | I | B | B | E |
| R | H | L | B | E | I | R | I | N | E | T | I | N | O | M |
| U | N | X | I | E | L | G | H | X | S | L | W | P | T | G |
| O | V | D | S | A | Q | O | H | U | I | A | Z | J | S | V |
| T | E | J | V | J | N | N | O | T | R | D | M | A | S | M |
| M | V | I | D | O | R | J | Y | R | N | Y | Y | G | E | F |
| P | H | I | U | S | M | B | I | C | O | U | R | A | G | E |
| C | V | R | X | H | W | O | X | Q | N | B | L | R | K | U |
| A | N | S | F | X | R | J | K | W | L | G | O | N | J | P |

# 94. Pastoral Encroachment

**20 per cent.** There are 25 field triangles with 5 of them bordering pastures along their long borders.

If you calculated the percentage, add **1 GRAIN** to your resources

# 95. Rescue Mission

|   | 1 | 0 | 4 | 0 | 0 | 4 | 0 | 2 |   |
|---|---|---|---|---|---|---|---|---|---|
| **1** |  |  |  |  | 🏠 | B |  |  | **1** |
| **1** |  |  | B |  |  |  |  |  | **1** |
| **2** |  |  | 🏠 |  |  | B | 🏠 | B | **2** |
| **1** |  | 🏠 | B |  |  |  |  | 🏠 | **1** |
| **2** | 🏠 |  |  |  |  | B | 🏠 | B | **2** |
| **2** | B | 🏠 | B |  |  | 🏠 |  |  | **2** |
| **1** |  |  | 🏠 |  | 🏠 | B |  |  | **1** |
| **1** |  |  | B |  |  |  |  |  | **1** |
|   | 1 | 0 | 4 | 0 | 0 | 4 | 0 | 2 |   |

If you rescued your allies, add **1 LUMBER** to your resources

# 96. Expert Advice

Two of the sages are experts on all three topics;
the third is an expert on none of them.

If you solved the puzzle, add **1 BRICK** to your resources

# 97. The Stone of Wisdom

The answer to the riddle is **"Shadow".** If you shift each of the letters
along the alphabet by the numbers given, the word **"Worthy"** is revealed:

| S | H | A | D | O | W |
|------|------|------|------|------|------|
| +4 | +7 | +16 | +16 | -7 | +2 |
| W | O | R | T | H | Y |

If you solved the riddle, add **1 BRICK** to your resources

# 98. Metropolis

If you linked the cities, add
**1 ORE**
to your resources

# 99. The Moonwalker Islands

| Island | Capital | Hazard | Trading |
|--------|---------|--------|---------|
| Myku | Aybisi | Pirates | Spices |
| Churmayn | Isle Bidair | Disease | Rubies |
| Jagki | Kunufleet | Storms | Silk |
| Tee-Tow | Delavu-sayif | War | Truffles |
| Mallon | Wonchaback | Corruption | Diamonds |

If you mapped the new islands, add **1 LUMBER** to your resources

# 100. The Final Word

**"Starting"!**

I
In
Sin
Sing
Sting
String
Staring
Starting

If you solved the riddle, add **1 CITY** to your achievements

# YOUR PUZZLE NOTES